I wish I had met him too — and I would have gone to St KILDA!

22/10/97.

With thanks to Comhairle Nan Eilean, which gave me a chance to live in the Western Isles and which can still deliver a better future for the people; with love to Cathleen who brought the Western Isles into my heart and my life; with gratitude for the forbearance of all my friends who live there; in affectionate memory of Werner Kissling who, with a touch of genius, opened a window on the Western Isles for the world.

And in hope for Cailean, that he will value the part of him that is Gaelic throughout his life.

A Poem of Remote Lives

A Poem of Remote Lives

THE ENIGMA OF WERNER KISSLING 1895-1988

Michael W Russell

Foreword by Gus Wylie

NEIL WILSON PUBLISHING • GLASGOW • SCOTLAND

SUPPORTED BY

THE POST OFFICE

© Michael W Russell, 1997

Published by Neil Wilson Publishing Ltd
303a The Pentagon Centre
36 Washington Street
GLASGOW
G3 8AZ

Tel: 0141-221-1117
Fax: 0141-221-5363
E-mail: nwp@cqm.co.uk
*http://*www.nwp.co.uk/

The author asserts his moral right to be identified as the author of this work

A CIP catalogue record for this book is available from the British Library.

ISBN 1-897784-46-5 (hardback)
ISBN 1-897784-78-3 (limpback)

The publisher gratefully acknowledges subsidy from the
Scottish Arts Council towards the publication of this volume.

Book design by Mark Blackadder

Graphic reproduction by Mitchell Graphics, Glasgow

Typeset in 10/14.5pt Bembo

Printed in UK by Bath Press

Contents

PART II

Examples of Kissling's photographs from his 1934
visit to Eriskay when he filmed *A Poem of Remote Lives*

APPENDICES

Preface

The fascinating and enigmatic life of Werner Kissling, born into enormous wealth in pre-Great War Germany and dying, nearly 93 years later in near poverty in his adopted country of Scotland, is a story worth telling and one well researched and told by Michael Russell in this biography. A key point of contact for us in Kissling's long and remarkable life, just as it initially was for the author himself, was his special place in 'Scottish' film and photography: above all with his unique record of real working life on Eriskay in 1934 – *A Poem of Remote Lives*.

Kissling's film was made at a time when John Grierson had established documentary film making at The Post Office and made the GPO Film Unit something of a legend in the history of film. Interestingly, just five years after Kissling's poetically evocative film, Maurice Harvey made a charming documentary called *The Islanders* about The Post Office's contribution to the life of three islands – Eriskay, Inner Farne and Guernsey, complete with snatches of Gaelic on the soundtrack, reminiscent of the earlier film.

More than half a century on from these pioneering films of the thirties, and notwithstanding the very real benefits of the telephone and opportunities for global communication and business via the Internet, The Post Office continues to keep islanders in touch with the rest of Scotland (and the world) through its letter and parcel services. There is also a community post office on Eriskay which adjoins the island's single shop run as a community co-operative.

Life on Eriskay, as in so many island and rural communities, is fragile as youngsters tend to drift away to cities for study and work. These communities have benefits as well as challenges and it is to be hoped that new ways of working and studying will provide young people with the opportunity to stay in these communities which become ever more important, imaginatively, at least, for us all.

Werner Kissling made only one film. Fortunately, we also have his photographic work which spanned some 60 years, many moving examples of which are reproduced in this book. As with his film, they were taken to accompany scholarly interests in ethnography but today will give great aesthetic and nostalgic pleasure for their eye on times past.

The headstone marking the grave of Werner Kissling in St Michael's Kirkyard in Dumfries sums up the life of this extraordinary and perhaps somewhat unfulfilled life of promise as: 'Soldier, Diplomat, Scholar, Gentleman'. Rightly, I think, Michael Russell feels 'Photographer and Film Maker' were needed to encapsulate his achievement better and this book is a very fitting tribute to a man to whom Scotland owes a small debt of gratitude.

JOHN WARD, CBE
Chairman, Scottish Post Office Board

Foreword

The photographs within this book serve to remind me of one of the unique attributes of the photographic process in that, unlike painting and drawing, it does not necessarily require a long apprenticeship before it can achieve its true worth. Therefore, in many ways, it has a unique potential for allowing the perceptive eye to show through, without the rigour of the studio and the limitations of the easel.

This was particularly so when the unique potential of the diminutive miniature camera became readily available to the itinerant photographer. No longer the need for the bulky tripod of the formative years of the medium, nor the use of cumbersome lights — instead, it allowed the compassionate worker to observe and quietly distil and record his or her response to the subject. Similarly, it allowed the enlightened 'amateur' to prevail and, in saying that, I should point out that this is in no way a pejorative remark - on the contrary, for the word 'amateur' stems from the Latin or French for 'love' and, from this stand point alone, there have been many fine workers within this area of endeavour whose photographs have stood the test of time.

Some of them were not even primarily photographers as such. I think particularly of Ben Shahn, the American illustrator, whose compassionate use of the Leica in the Dust Bowl of the American South was to produce such a memorable batch of images; or those of Vishniac in the Polish ghettos as the storms of war gathered in the late 1930s; or the lyrical images of Lartigue in France and England; and for the bulk of the 20th century, the New Orleans images of Storyville by EJ Bellocq, and especially, the magical images of her black neighbourhood by Eudora Welty, the distinguished writer of Southern prose. And in the Hebridean context, of course, there was Margaret Fay Shaw, and 'Herself' - MEM Donaldson. All of them were driven by compassion and concern for the individual, and all with a story to tell.

For me, Werner Kissling's images have that similar and singular quality - a quiet compassionate look at a subject that he loved, without exploitation, or patronising aloofness, which allows us later to examine the content almost as an archaeologist would look at an excavation in a field. His concern for aspects of ethnology and genealogy was the perfect basis upon which to make his fine portraits.

The small camera and its almost silent shutter allowed him to work quietly and with sensitivity and the subjects responded accordingly and we, in turn, find ourselves looking at small details within the frame: the shoes, or lack of them, the details of the croft in the background, the knitting of the sweater, the elements of physiognomy and countenance, of gesture and returned empathy. Not for Kissling the route of the propagandist, but, instead, the culling together of an infinitely precious and ultimately irreplaceable collection of images that afford us a unique insight into a singular way of life at a particular period of time - one which will not return.

But for us, we can be thankful that the camera was there, and that the shutter was tripped and, some 60 years on, we can return to these images again and again, and savour their unique quality and warmth with affection and relish.

St Albans, *August 1997*

MICHAEL RUSSELL

Acknowledgements

This is not an academic biography, or a lifetime historical study. I am not a professional biographer, and when one is dealing with a man who valued his privacy and who prided himself on leaving so little behind, then the resources and detective work necessary to reconstruct a life are likely to be beyond a part-time writer who finds no difficulty in filling his days with the minutiae of politics.

Catriona MacKinnon, originally from Eriskay, also assisted greatly with the identification of people in Kissling's photos and in the film, as did the people of Eriskay at a community ceilidh in 1995.

What this book sets out to do is to publish some of the marvellous photographs taken by an intriguing individual and to lay out enough of the background of the photographer to allow his work to be appreciated anew and to be set in the context of his remarkable life.

It is also a personal account of the way in which I have been involved with the story of Werner Kissling, and with his ideas, for the best part of 20 years.

It could not have been written without the work of Werner Kissling, nor without the devotion to him and his memory of his executor David Lockwood. He has allowed access to Kissling's photographs and helped over the past three years, firstly with a BBC 2 documentary about Kissling and then with this book. Many of Dr Kissling's friends have also given generously of their time, recollections and insights, motivated by their affection for him which is always impressive and gives the best clue to his character. His family, and particularly his great-nephew Bolko Kissling have also been a source of some vital information.

Janet McBain, the archivist of the Scottish Film Archive, introduced me to Kissling and helped me find information on him when I started my research, and she has always been great company, no matter the problems I bring her. Margaret MacKelvie of *Comataidh Telebhisein Gaidhling* was enthusiastic from the start of the documentary project that proceeded this book and helped to secure the necessary funding for research. Ken MacQuarrie of BBC Scotland commissioned the film and encouraged me to think about a book, as did his colleague Donalda MacKinnon.

The School of Scottish Studies, in the person of its Director Dr Margaret MacKay and its Photo Librarian Ian MacKenzie has also been very supportive and helpful, and the school's permission to reproduce photographs from their collection is gratefully acknowledged. The Royal Gourock Yacht Club was able to provide information on Kissling's chartered yacht, although not, alas, on its crew and I am grateful to its Honorary Secretary for such speedy attention to my odd request!

Dr Albert Ridgeley of Leica Camera Ltd was an invaluable source of information on Kissling's camera, the Leica III, and he has kindly contributed a brief history of his company and the camera on page 108.

I am particularly indebted to The Post Office for its generous support of this book. Not only does it bring my letters all the way up a 500-yard track but also by assisting books such as this shows its deep involvement in the history and traditions of rural Scotland. Given the pace of rural change - and often decline - the Post Office's continuing role in our countryside is one we should defend and cherish.

My principal collaborators on the documentary – Ishbel MacIver and Flora Thomson – have been the mainstays of both that project and the additional work required to start, continue and finish the story I wanted to write. They brought their usual enthusiasm and commitment to Kissling and became as addicted as I am to his life and work. They are the vital components of what I think of as the perfect production team, and I hope to work with them again in the future.

Finally my wife Cathleen and son Cailean have borne the brunt not just of this book, but of the documentary and of all the other things I give myself to and which takes time away from them. They should know that I am always conscious of how much they support me and how badly I often seem to support them. The balance can only be made up with love.

Moran Taing gu dhearabh.

Feorlean, Argyll, *July 1997*

Three Aspects of Kissling

Here are three brief entries about Werner Kissling that have not yet appeared in any reference book. First, the biographical:

KISSLING, Dr Werner Fridrich Theodor; b: April 11, 1895, Heizendorf, nr Breslau, Silesia, (then in Germany, now Poland); d: February 3, 1988, Moorheads Nursing Home, Dumfries, Scotland.

Ethnologist, film maker, photographer. Ed: Gymnasium of St Mary Magdelene, Breslau; Gymnasium, Leobschutz; Freidrich-Wilhelm University, Berlin; Alberts University, Königsberg; Consular School, Vienna; Cambridge University. Military service in the Prussian Guards (1914) and the German Navy (1915-18). Consular Service for the Weimar Republic from 1919-31, stationed in Riga, Geneva (including attachment to the German delegation, League of Nations) Madrid, Budapest, and London.

Fellow of the Royal Geographical Society (1930), Fellow of the Royal Anthropological Institute (1931).

Interned in the Tower of London and on the Isle of Man (1939-42). Proprietor, Kings Arms Hotel, Melrose (until mid-1960s). Honorary Assistant, Dumfries Museum (1969-88). Publications: The Hebridean Black House (Man), numerous articles and photos in Scottish and other publications (1956-1984). Unmarried, no children.

Second, the creative:

Werner Kissling has a unique place in Scottish film history: he shot and directed the first ever film using the Gaelic language. He also deserves an honourable mention in the history of Scottish photography.

A wealthy German aristocrat, he was influenced by his mother's interest in photography and by her visit to the Western Isles of Scotland in 1905. The first of his photographs that still exist were taken in Riga in 1919, when he was attached to the German consular and military administration. Whilst working in the diplomatic service of the Weimar Republic he was involved in the prosecution of Hitler after the 'Beer Hall Putsch' and was later posted to London where he developed links with Cambridge University in pursuit of his studies in ethnology. His particular area of interest was the Hebridean black house and, having left the German diplomatic service in 1931, he pursued a life of scholarship and gentility (affected by his impoverishment in the early 1960s) until he died in 1988 in Dumfries, Scotland.

In connection with his research he visited the Western Isles (and especially the island of Eriskay) on many occasions between the early thirties and sixties. In 1934 he spent a summer on Eriskay and took a large number of photographs. He also brought with him a 35mm film camera and recorded a number of scenes of traditional island life which were edited together into a 20-minute black and white film, released in 1935 under the title *A Poem of Remote Lives*.

The film not only features Gaelic song (recorded for him in London by the London Gaelic Choir) but also sections of Gaelic conversation, some of which were probably recorded on the island. The film was gifted by Kissling to the School of Scottish Studies in Edinburgh and transferred by them, in 1979, to the Scottish Film Archive where it has become a standard source of footage of the pre-war Western Isles.

Although he never made another film, he continued to take photographs until he was almost 90, recording many traditional crafts in places as diverse as New Zealand, Yorkshire and the Solway Firth. He also assisted Dumfries Museum in collecting traditional artefacts.

Though naturally gregarious and with a wide circle of acquaintances, Kissling had few close friends and expressed a desire that he and his work should not be the subject of study. Just before he died in 1988 he appointed the curator of Dumfries Museum, David Lockwood, as his executor and bequeathed to him a small collection of personal papers and family photographs, as well as a set of original lantern slides of Eriskay taken in 1934. Kissling was habitually selling photographs and negatives in the 30 years before his death, and as well as a sizeable collection in Dumfries Museum, there are hundreds of frames of negative film in the School of Scottish Studies in Edinburgh, as well as other examples of his work in the Royal Scottish Museum, the Museum of Mankind and in a number of other collections. He also gave photographs to friends.

Although Dumfries Museum hosted two small exhibitions of his work in the seventies and early eighties, his contribution to film and photography in Scotland has remained largely unrecorded. A new print of his film was prepared by the Scottish Film Archive in 1997 and work is planned to restore its soundtrack.

And finally, the personal:

Dr Werner Fridrich Theodor Kissling has been in my mind, and in my life, for the best part of 18 years. For the first nine of those he was alive and living not a hundred miles from where I grew up and not 50 from where I was living. And yet I never met him.

When he died in Dumfries in February 1988 he was only seven years shy of his 100th birthday. His life had started in a castle in Silesia, then part of a very Prussian Germany. It had included both army and navy service in the First World War, a diplomatic and civil service career, great wealth and great poverty and an academic record which is only now being brought to light. It had also included a remarkable series of achievements in photography and a single, historical film.

It was that film that kept Werner Kissling in my head and my imagination. It was that film that stayed with me, being replayed in my mind time and time again. And it was the story of the making of that film that lead me first to make a television documentary, and then to write, about Werner Kissling and his life.

This book is, in part, the story of how I have been able to write these definitions and about my own search for an unknown film maker. And it is also a personal homage to someone whose life and work deserves to be remembered again.

PART I

Under the Distinguished Patronage of

H.R.H. THE PRINCE OF WALES

Lord of the Isles

who has graciously consented to be present if possible.

H.R.H. THE DUKE OF YORK	H.R.H. THE DUCHESS OF YORK
Earl of Inverness	Countess of Inverness

Patrons:

THE PRIME MINISTER

THE MARQUIS OF LONDONDERRY, K.G., M.V.O., P.C.	THE MARCHIONESS OF LONDONDERRY, D.B.E.
THE EARL OF DUNMORE, V.C., D.S.O.	THE COUNTESS OF DUNMORE

SIR DONALD CAMERON OF LOCHIEL, K.T., C.M.G., D.L.

MACLEOD OF MACLEOD, K.C.B.	RT. HON. SIR GODFREY COLLINS, M.P.

A Hebridean Evening

will be held at

LONDONDERRY HOUSE

(kindly lent by the Marquis and Marchioness of Londonderry)

Tuesday, 30th April, 1935

at 9.30 p.m.

> PRE-VIEW OF THE FILM
>
> ## "ERISKAY"
>
> ### A POEM OF REMOTE LIVES
>
> shortly to be released

Mr. DUNCAN M. MORISON

who has collected the Songs and composed the Introductory Music for this very beautiful record of Island life, will accompany at the Piano the Solo renderings of SYDNEY MacEWAN

THE LONDON GAELIC CHOIR

(Conducted by Mr. JOHN S. MacINTYRE)

will give a programme of Hebridean Songs

SOLOISTS:

Miss MOLLY WILSON   Mr. ALEXANDER MacRAE

As the space in Lady Londonderry's beautiful house is limited, it is advisable to obtain tickets as soon as possible

Tickets, One Guinea and 10s. 6d.

may be obtained from:

The COUNTESS OF DUNMORE, 17 Cleveland Gardens, W.2. Tel.: Paddington 1446.	Mrs. IAIN HILLEARY, Sandford Manor, Woodley, Berkshire.	Mrs. NORMAN STEWART, 99 Fillebrook Road, Leytonstone.
Miss MEREDITH, Londonderry House, Park Lane, W.1. Tel.: Grosvenor 1616.	Mrs. HUGH M. MATHESON, 46 Prince's Gardens, S.W.7. Tel.: Kensington 8332.	Mrs. ARTHUR T. MacMILLAN, 17 Cheyne Gardens, S.W.3. Tel.: Flaxman 9495.

The Hon. Treasurer,
Mr. JOHN MacLEOD,
75 Prebend Gardens, W.6.
Tel.: Riverside 3902.

The entire net proceeds of the Evening will be used to help the people of the Island of Eriskay to provide wool for spinning and weaving

Ed. Hughes & Co. (D. G. Lusty), Printers, 12 Well Court, E.C.4

CHAPTER 1

Introduction to a Film

The story of my search for Kissling starts on the island of South Uist in the spring of 1979. For the past 19 months I had been the director of a community film and video project, called in Gaelic *Cinema Sgire*[1], based in the southern part of the Western Isles. I had been involved in film and video from my third year at the University of Edinburgh. During that year I had changed career, giving up what I thought was a calling to the Episcopal Priesthood in a welter of family recrimination and the inevitable sense of personal failure. My change in university course, and my abrupt departure from the cloistered life of the Episcopal Theological College in Edinburgh, meant that I had to spend six months at home at Troon in Ayrshire. I was a somewhat ill-fitting, returned, 19-year old for whom the fatted calf was definitely not going to an early roasting.

I needed a job and in those days of bountiful employment I quickly found one as a ranger in the Culzean Country Park where a new visitor centre was about to open. My aptitude for interpreting the wildlife of South Ayrshire was not great – but my National Trust boss quickly realised that I had an aptitude for sound and pictures, and I was set to work helping to design and develop the opening programme for the centre's then technologically-advanced audio-visual presentation.

I got the production bug immediately, and on returning to university to finish a course in Scottish History and Literature, set my sights on working in the media.

After university my mix of experience quickly got me a position producing audio-visual programmes for the Church of Scotland (turning down a final board for a trainee's post in BBC Radio on the way – an opportunity that I have only occasionally paused to regret). The Church of Scotland post was based in their headquarters in Edinburgh, a grim building that was called by the staff – not affectionately – the Lubyanka of George Street. For three years I produced and directed, moving on to video and even

dipping my fingers in the expensive medium of film. It was a good training, with a lot of freedom to experiment as long as the client departments in the Church didn't realise that was what I was doing. At the same time I dabbled in radio and in the issue of community access and choice in the media.

I also got interested in Gaelic, first through a study of Scottish poetry and then by hovering in the haunts of the Gael in Edinburgh, including the famous West End Hotel. In mid-1977 I spotted in *The Scotsman* an advertisement for a new post directing a video and film project in the Western Isles, which was based on the theory of community access and production. Every man and woman a producer, every child a sound recordist and cameraman, and every production authentic and relevant. It was a heady notion, and one that 20 years later is not much further to fruition – although real-time broadcasting via the Internet holds tantalising opportunities for the 21st century.

The job matched both of my principal interests, and the prospect of leaving Edinburgh held no fears. I applied, and greatly to my surprise, got the job; although my Gaelic, then and now, is far from fluent and my local connections were non-existent. Maybe I sold myself well, or was lucky, but at just 24 I became the director of a project with international significance. My new role was placed within a web of highly original and thoughtful initiatives in community development which were the brainchild of Dr Finlay MacLeod, who was then a senior figure in education in the Western Isles and is still an inspiration to those who want the best of change for the islands and the Gaelic community.

The story of those projects needs to be told, but somewhere else. They came, they tried and then went, but each in their own way left a legacy that did not die during the inimical years of Thatcherite denigration of 'society' and its better communal feelings. At their height they were invigorating to work in, and I hope invigorating to be around. They both profited from, and suffered, the brash enthusiasms of a young and idealistic staff, for whom the hothouse atmosphere of community development in a remote area was as

---

[1] Best translated as 'Community Cinema'.

much an ideological commitment as a job.

Cinema Sgire both made programmes (on open-reel half-inch video in a format that now seems technologically in the Stone Age) and showed them, along with feature films and a host of other material. We maintained and operated a cinema circuit for performances that covered ten inhabited islands. We travelled in a van or on a boat with projectors, televisions, screens, spare bulbs and a bulging bag of tapes and reels which could and did include the latest epic from the primary school in Iochdar, along with a Hollywood blockbuster, always past its first flush of profitable commercial release.

In time it was obvious that it was Hollywood that held the most appeal, particularly as most people were only just trading up from 425-line black and white television with one channel. There were notable mistakes in programming, such as choosing *Jonathan Livingstone Seagull* as the first ever film shown on the Island of Berneray, a mistake brought home at the end of the performance as a deadly silence fell on the packed audience in a Nissen hut, broken by a single sad comment – 'Nice film, but we do see lots of seagulls here anyway.' But there were also notable successes – especially *Whisky Galore* which could be shown on Barra at any hour of the day and night and still require at least two encore performances just to satisfy the queue which had formed well before the film started.

Another regular favourite was a presentation of archive films of the Western Isles. *Cinema Sgire* was supported by the Scottish Film Council which had initiated the project and the archivist of the council, Janet McBain, would visit the project about once every six months to undertake an evening of archive presentations, with me working, as usual, as the projectionist.

It was at one of these in the late spring of 1979 that she showed a film that had just been gifted to the archive by the School of Scottish Studies at Edinburgh University. Due to reorganisation of their collection of materials, they were passing on to the Film Archive any moving pictures of relevance.

The film was called *A Poem of Remote Lives*.

It is hard sometimes to remember the first impact of a film, or a book, or a poem. I recall only two things about that evening at Iochdar in South Uist when I saw Kissling's film. The first is walking on the beach at Ardivachar after the performance, on a perfect evening. Janet and I and one or two others went there after the film performance because Janet had never seen a real, lengthy and spectacular sunset in the Western Isles. (It is on Ardivachar granite that the copy of the Doomsday Book, gifted to the USA on its bicentenary, sits in Washington – not just because it is virtually the nearest inhabited point of Britain to America, but because it was also the first key point that pilots of lend-lease planes saw as they approached the country during the Second World War).

The second was what Janet has told me about the film by way of introduction. She had been told that it had been made by a German émigré,

a diplomat who had been based at the German Embassy in London. She knew that he was still alive, and living in Dumfries, but that he had recently been ill.

I had looked at, and indeed shown to audiences, a number of other films of the Western Isles that the archive held, but none had struck me as remotely accurate or sympathetic in their portrayal of Gaelic life. The 1923 film of St Kilda – at that time the only film portraying the island as inhabited – had captions that ridiculed the islanders and their way of life. Promotional films from the 1930s, 40s and 50s – usually for Caledonian MacBrayne – veered between the embarrassing and the patronising.

Kissling's film was different. Even today, having seen it probably hundreds of times, it seems very close to the people it portrays. Kissling's camera observes and records – it takes no stance outside the immediacy of being there. The script, whilst English in tone and sometimes slightly supercilious in approach, is clearly well-informed and is counterpointed by Gaelic song and some rather muffled conversations in Gaelic.

As a student of history I had always asked myself the question – what was it like to be there: in 18th-century Scotland or in Viking Norway, or on the Clyde steamers at the turn of the century? This film seemed to convey to the audience precisely what it was like to live on a small Hebridean island in 1934.

The film was shown at least twice more on the *Cinema Sgire* circuit, and one of those showings was on the island of Eriskay itself. The audience for the film there had a great deal more information on Kissling and some personal memories of his visit. He had arrived in the early summer on a white yacht, along with at least one male companion, referred to by the locals as 'the valet'. He had lodged on the island for a couple of months, and taken both his movie film camera (35mm) and a stills camera everywhere he went. At least one person had a black and white print of a photograph by Kissling, and a number of individuals could name some of those who appeared in the film.

I left the Western Isles in 1982, and moved to Inverness to run on a full-time basis the Celtic Film and Television Festival which I had started in 1980. I had the vague idea of bringing together film and television workers who were using minority languages in their work, or who were involved in community initiatives like *Cinema Sgire*.

The forty five film and television professionals who gathered as delegates to the first festival in Iochdar, South Uist in the second week of April 1980 (ten days after my marriage to a local teacher from North Uist, who had a most unusual honeymoon!) took part in a seminar and a series of screenings that stretched from the Butt of Lewis to the Island of Vatersay, south of Barra – screenings that included Kissling's film. Late at night in the bar of the Lochboisdale Hotel they also resolved – prior to the largest member of the Welsh contingent falling backwards into a drunken sleep and having to be manhandled up the stairs to bed – that there must be a second festival which, despite funding crisis after funding crisis, was held at Harlech in North Wales in 1981. By the time of the third event – in Wexford, Ireland – the organisation of the festival was my full-time occupation, and *Cinema Sgire* had fallen victim to the rise of the Tories: it survived just as a voluntary cinema circuit for only a few more years.

Within one year, (and after a difference of opinion on what the festival should be doing, a difference of opinion made critical by the whip hand of the television funders), I was working in Glasgow in what I believed was a temporary job in charge of a small media support company – a job that was eventually to last almost eight years and allow me to build Network Scotland to a flourishing enterprise employing over 70 staff. The festival continued through bad times and good, and I rejoined the Executive Committee again in 1990, surviving virtual expulsion from the event's parent body for a set of radical views (again about what the festival should do and who it should attract) that were far from popular with those in mainstream television who now signed the cheques.

During those eight years Kissling and his film came into my mind on many occasions. In 1988 I read a brief obituary of him in *The Scotsman* and was astonished to discover that he had been alive until then. I had also seen the film used on television either as a brief illustration of pre-war life in the Western Isles, or sometimes even as unattributed archive footage conjuring up a remote Hebridean past.

With the creation of *Comataidh Telebhisein Gaidhlig* (CTG) in 1990 there came the opportunity for those who were involved with Gaelic and who had experience or ambition in television to create new structures and new programmes. I had been involved with Gaelic and the aspirations of Gaelic television since the establishment of *Cinema Sgire* in 1977 and I decided that I couldn't resist the temptation to go back to production and Gaelic. In 1991 I started my own production company, *Eala Bhan*[2], and one of the first ideas I developed was for a film on Kissling and his story.

The idea was knocked back on two occasions by the CTG and whilst everyone I spoke to about the story was enthusiastic, their enthusiasm was never manifested in a commission. It was not until Spring 1994 – almost 15 years to the day after I had first heard Kissling's name and seen his film – that I received approval for a research project which would develop a full proposal for a documentary on Werner Kissling.

Enthusiasm is a roller coster – it goes down as well as up. Getting a research and development commission for a film is not the same as getting the money to make it, but for a few days and weeks the enthusiasm for the idea (which has taken several batterings in the fight even for development funding), returns and the fun of research and finding out keeps the adrenalin flowing.

The starting point for the search for Kissling had to lie with the film and particularly with the person who had first introduced me to it. Some months earlier Janet had provided a copy of the film for me to use to persuade Margaret MacKelive of CTG to fund the development. Margaret's family were from Eriskay and she too had been overpowered by its direct simplicity. She had shown the film to her father, who had recognised his brother as a young man – a recognition that was, in her words, like a powerful shock to him. I now needed a copy of the film for myself and arranged to see Janet to collect a VHS transfer, copies of any documentation that she might have on the film and to see the film myself once again.

My search for Werner Kissling was about to begin.

---

[2] White Swan, named not only after the ever present birds of Uist, but also a famous North Uist 20th-century love song.

KISSLING'S SUITCASE, FILLED WITH HIS REMAINING PERSONAL EFFECTS, AS IT APPEARED IN THE BBC2
DOCUMENTARY BROADCAST ON JANUARY 11, 1996.

CHAPTER 2

Searching for Kissling

In the world of television no matter how much you enjoy or are good at one job, you have to be able to do several: the polite term for spreading oneself so thinly is 'multiskilling'.

I enjoy research more than anything, although film editing comes a close second. But both of those activities are labour intensive and therefore expensive. Modern television also requires an ability to do as much as possible with as little as possible. The initial research for the film that was broadcast by BBC2 on January 11, 1996 had to be done in a period of two months in the summer of 1994 and subsequent information was gleaned in research time snatched from other projects and between episodes in my other life as a political hack running a General Election campaign for the Scottish National Party.

In an ideal world the time for research would be almost unlimited and the resources to travel, talk and buy the time to think, would be freely available. But this is not an ideal world and accordingly the search for Kissling has been neither complete nor exhaustive. From time to time a friend or acquaintance will bring back information from a casual meeting that adds a new dimension to Kissling, or places him in North Uist or Argyll in a particular year on which I have only sketchy information. These incidents usually make me realise how hard it is to know comprehensively about anybody – and indeed there are parts of Kissling's life about which I have, and can find, little or no information. In the late forties he certainly spent time in Argyll, but the early sixties are also largely undocumented as his hotel venture failed and he began to face life without any continuing financial support.

On other occasions a contact would not return my phone calls, or would be reluctant to talk, for reasons that can only be guessed at. Perhaps it was the approach, or the seemingly impertinent attempt to define a man who told all his close friends that he did not want to be written or talked about. Perhaps also, given Kissling's sexuality and private life, it is a defence mechanism, an unwillingness to reveal aspects not just of Kissling, but of the individual who knew him. Whatever the reasons, the search has been at times frustrating, at times annoying, but also at times highly satisfying. Yet what has emerged has frequently opened new areas for exploration rather than completing the portrait.

Trying to tell something of his story, and to show his work to a wider audience, I have been able to flesh out some of the detail of his life. But, as I stated in the introduction, this is not an exhaustive academic biography due to pressure of available time, lack of resource and my primary intention. My portrait of Kissling is designed to let those who come to his work for the first time understand a little about the type of man he was and what drove him – and that is hard enough, because he was secretive, enigmatic and intensely private. It is also a personal homage to someone who has given me great pleasure and allowed me to understand something more about the Western Isles and its past – an abiding interest fuelled by collecting some of the many books (good, bad and indifferent) on the islands that have been written to confound Dr Johnson's reported view of St Kilda that a place with so little of man and so much of nature could not possibly provide the stimulation required for creativity and human progress.

My portrait is also an expression of my fascination with a life that was so out of the ordinary: a life that seems to be tragic in its scope and intensity, and yet which appears to have been lived with great satisfaction and not a little fulfilment. The life of Werner Kissling is, quite simply, a great story – yet one that would be easier to fictionalise and tell in that way, than to understand and touch in reality. Weaving into its fabric those who have helped to tell it, has also proved to be difficult. Accordingly, before we start on Kissling himself – and we will start by looking at and trying to understand his one film, which is his unique achievement – it is necessary to finish the story of how it has come to be told.

The Scottish Film Archive not only holds a print of *A Poem Of Remote Lives*, but also some supporting documentation on the film which Janet McBain had gathered because of her own interest in Kissling. Reviews, published on its première, and a photocopy of the original poster for that showing, lie on the file. Janet herself had found out a little more about him, including the fact that he was a prominent anti-Nazi and that he had a long association with Dumfries Museum. The Scottish Film Archive had first brought the film to my attention, so the search had to start there.

As I began the research on Kissling in the summer of 1994 I recalled that Allan MacDonald of *Media Nan Eilean* was not only from Eriskay, but had told me that he had met Kissling. He had also provided Janet with background information and Allan was, as ever, happy to talk and share his experience: his father had known Kissling in the 1930s on Eriskay and Allan had visited Werner in Dumfries shortly before his death. He described a deeply moving discussion, when Werner's love for the islands and its people had shone through.

Research is often a matter of spreading the widest possible net, and seeing what is trawled up in it. I visited Dumfries Library which held a file of cuttings and some material on a public subscription for Werner's gravestone which was erected some two years after his death. That file led me to David Lockwood, the curator of Dumfries Museum, who turned out to be Werner's executor. He in turn had addresses and phone numbers for a number of Werner's friends who had contributed to the subscription and a contact number for a nephew of Werner's who he thought was still alive in Hamburg.

Intriguingly, David also had a suitcase full of Werner's personal effects. I first looked at it in David's spare room in his red sandstone Dumfries townhouse and it revealed a wealth of papers and photographs relating to Werner's life, family and friends. In the museum itself there were not only artefacts that Werner had collected for display but also boxes of negatives and papers, drafts of articles, carefully prepared explanatory sheets of contact prints about all sorts of crafts in the Scottish Borders and in West Yorkshire and even some material that related to the Western Isles and his film, including the original handwritten script.

But perhaps most importantly of all, David had two wooden boxes of glass-plate lantern slides, the originals of the photographs that Werner had taken in Eriskay and South Uist in 1934, and on some subsequent visits.

David's contacts led me to others: Andrew Croft who had letters and photographs and a lifetime of memories (although some rather imperialistic antagonism to Gaelic, as we were to discover when the final documentary was made); Craig Meyer who collected photographs and helped Werner financially, as well as maintaining a friendship that was much valued; the MacLellan brothers who, as children in South Uist, had all known Werner as he had been a regular part of their lives and a help when they needed someone; Ralph Coleman in Dumfries who had listened to 'The Doctor's' stories and who had devised the segmentation of his life that was to appear on his tombstone and which I have used, in part, in this book.

In addition to contacting these people, Werner's nephew led me on to Werner's great-nephew, Bolko Kissling, who was able to tell me something of his family history but whose interest in his uncle was coloured by the dispute that had essentially cut Werner off from his relatives for half a century.

The family had no idea that their relative – whom they undoubtedly saw as the black sheep of the family – had been, or might be, of any interest to the wider world. Bolko and his father knew nothing of the Eriskay film, and little about Werner's photography.

My investigations in Melrose, and the period of Werner's ownership of the Kings Arms Hotel, were not as productive. The man who bought the hotel from Kissling didn't really want to talk about him and it was impossible to find the Mr Lawson who had been the hotel manager and whose friendship with Werner seemed to have gone very sour. Of those who could remember Kissling in Melrose, none could, or would, give anything more than the sketchiest of accounts – and the few good memories (particularly of Werner playing host in the bar to his friends) were the only tangible elements of the story.

Official sources were patchy too: the German Foreign Ministry's record of Werner's career closes in 1931 – a difficulty for the claims that Werner told of his departure from the German diplomatic service under Hitler's threats in 1933. The Museum of Mankind in London had photographs from New Zealand but nothing more, and Cambridge University only had records of his work on the Hebridean black house.

The School of Scottish Studies in Edinburgh had much of the material which was duplicated in Dumfries (early on it became apparent that Werner made much from little: a single photograph could be sold in print form again and again) and one or two other collections had material which I had seen elsewhere. Despite several attempts to find memories of Kissling in New Zealand, nothing was forthcoming.

There were others too who had a memory or a photograph, but no more. Slowly – and with a growing sense of excitement as letters were answered or phone calls returned – I began to get a fuller picture of Werner Kissling and became convinced that there was enough information to justify a documentary. I prepared a full report on the research, together with a proposal and costing for a single half-hour film and submitted the whole package to the CTG in September 1994. Two months later they decided to fund the programme, but there was no commission from a broadcaster until early 1995, when Ken MacQuarrie of BBC Scotland agreed to a developed proposal for a single half-hour documentary to be transmitted in early January 1996.

However, just as the CTG's agreement was given I agreed to take on the post of Chief Executive of the Scottish National Party, at least until the next general election. Accordingly whatever work I could do on the documentary was going to be circumscribed by other duties and I abandoned the idea of directing the project myself. But I had no hesitation in asking Ishbel MacIver, the best of the modern Gaelic television directors, if she would undertake the task. Her collaboration (later joined by Flora Thomson as co-producer and general organiser) meant that the film would still be true to my early ideas and yet enhanced immeasurably by the caring and inspirational talents of these others.

Work on the documentary started in the early summer of 1995 and filming took place in September and October of that year. Ishbel, Flora and I spent long evenings discussing what we wanted to achieve and how to achieve it: we reviewed all the research, talked again to those who had provided information and assessed the development of the story at every turn.

Choosing a crew to get the right visual style and the commitment needed to any independent production took time. I wanted Andy MacLeod as cameraman, as I had worked with him on several occasions and found his eye for pictures to be as close to my vision as it was possible to get. His brash and hustling style was something I had got used to, and even valued, and Ishbel finally agreed that he was right for the job, just as I agreed that Becky Thomson would provide the quality of sound we needed.

The choice of those to take part in any documentary is often self-limiting: not everyone can even answer interview questions coherently. In addition, from the very start I had seen the documentary as being a Gaelic-language programme, and whilst it is possible (and necessary) to use English speakers from time to time, the balance of the story had to be in Gaelic and directed at a Gaelic audience in the first instance.

Language choice is not just a matter of where the funding can come from. For too long it has been assumed that stories about Gaelic can easily be told in English, for the convenience of the majority. This, at least in its first incarnation, was a story that belonged to the Gael – the story of the first film ever to use Gaelic, of the man who made it and recorded some of the strongest modern historical images of Gaelic life. It was not only appropriate that Gaelic was the medium for exploring Kissling – it was necessary if the project was to contribute something to Eriskay and all those Gaelic speakers who might watch it.

The final schedule involved shooting in Edinburgh, London, Dumfries and Eriskay, as well as in Breslau – now part of Poland. Within days of starting shooting Ishbel decided she needed more time and more resources and despite my initial reluctance to seek an increased budget, CTG agreed comparatively readily to provide additional finance so that the story could be broader and more visual than we had first planned.

The film was edited over a period of months at Picardy Television in Edinburgh, and the appointed BBC executive producer, Donalda MacKinnon, saw two different cuts and made a series of suggestions, some of which were taken on board as the final edit came into being. The final choice of what to say and what to leave out is always a difficult one with any single documentary, but the material that Ishbel had shot with Bolko Kissling was particularly strong and drove the story forward, as was the recording of a ceilidh in Eriskay at which Kissling's slides had been shown. Ishbel had also been drawn to the musical aspects of Kissling – who was a keen listener, though not a performer – and wanted to use as much music as possible.

Our first choice of a narrative voice was the former head of Gaelic and editor of BBC Radio Scotland, Neil Fraser, but although he was interested in doing the recording, a conflict of dates (and perhaps some nervousness about working with me after many years of ideological difference and not a few disputes) made him drop out. Chris Dillon substituted in his usual professional manner, although his voice was perhaps a little light for the script, which was constantly being developed by Ishbel, Flora and myself.

At the same time I was arranging a preview of the programme in Dumfries which took place only days before Ishbel went on a extended trip to South Africa. A small audience who knew Kissling saw the film in the compact theatre of the Burns Centre on the banks of the Nith and there was an emotional response. Even Ralph Coleman – who had repeatedly indicated that Kissling was against having his life exposed in this way – was enthusiastic and felt that 'The Doctor' might not have minded such a sympathetic portrait.

The film's transmission on January 11, 1996 at 7.00pm on BBC2 was preceded by a lengthy article in the *Spectrum* supplement of *Scotland on Sunday* in late December and, on the day, by a good preview in *The Scotsman* which made it their 'Choice of the Day'. It was not nearly as well reviewed by the *West Highland Free Press*, although that approach may have been more than a little coloured by political antagonism. The transmission brought half a dozen letters of approval, some phone calls from individuals who remembered Kissling and a rash of complaints to the BBC about their method of subtitling on Ceefax, which meant that a number of greatly frustrated people without Teletext had not been able to understand a word of it.

Some weeks before transmission Sheila Hamilton (a colleague with whom I undertook some public relations work) had introduced me to the Glasgow-based publisher Neil Wilson who expressed an interest in viewing the photographs and in the possibility of creating a book on Kissling. That development was agreed to in February 1996 with a proposed publication date in the autumn – a date that was postponed twice as political events crowded out the allocation of any meaningful time I had to write.

Selection and reduction is the art of television production: expansion and development is what is necessary for a book based on any television programme, and starting again to look at Kissling it has been necessary to revisit sources, check information again and try to fill in some of the gaps which inevitably a half-hour documentary failed to address.

It was also necessary to try and re-focus on Kissling himself, and in particular on his single film. For the story of Werner Kissling started, for me, with his film and in telling his story to others it is more than appropriate to start there too.

THE *ELSPETH* NEARS ERISKAY. A STILL REPRODUCED FROM THE FILM *A POEM OF REMOTE LIVES*.

CHAPTER 3

A Poem of Remote Lives

There are many ways to look at films but one of the best is to sit at an old Steenbeck editing machine and let it run through the small viewer between the plates. I had viewed Kissling's film before, but the first time I saw it in the film archive it was on such an editing machine and that is the way that film becomes real. Kissling's film runs for just under 20 minutes – it is about 2000 feet in length in the 35mm film stock that Kissling used.

That length itself provides the first mystery, because there are indications at the earliest stages of the film's editing in London that the final version would be 3000 feet long – running to about half an hour. Janet McBain – who has seen the film almost as often as I have – believes that the ending is unusually abrupt and that there may have been a longer version in existence at some stage. During the making of the Kissling documentary I fantasised about finding this longer version in an attic room belonging to one of his friends in London, or in one of the many boxes of his photographs that are stored in the basement of Dumfries Museum. No such film ever appeared, and of course the off-cuts from his original shooting must have long since been dumped or destroyed during the war.

The 2000 feet we have today – even in the copies that have been made by the Scottish Film Archive – have some small blemishes. In particular the soundtrack is muffled and it is difficult to make out the detail of conversation in the background of some scenes[1]. It is to be hoped that future generations can get an even better view of the island of Eriskay in 1934 than we have had – thanks to technical developments that Kissling could not have even dreamt of.

The film opens with the certificate of the British Board of Film Censors – passed for 'Universal Exhibition', in other words a modern-day 'U' certificate. This indicates that the film was intended for public viewing and for commercial distribution. The film appeared in the Zenifilms catalogue shortly after its completion and would have been used as a 'filler', or short first

film, in some of the many thousands of cinemas in Britain that were doing a roaring trade in the mid-30s. The usual fate of such films was to move from commercial venues, through private and rural film shows, down to the educational section of the market and the ultimately out-of-the-catalogue and into-the-dustbin of film history. The prestigious *Monthly Film Bulletin* for September 1935 presages this decline by categorising the film's suitability as being for 'geography and rural interests classroom film for all over 12'.

After the certificate the picture fades to black and the soundtrack starts with the opening words of the first verse of a song called Island Moon:
Tonight there is a restlessness in the wind . . .

The title of the film – *Eriskay: A Poem Of Remote Lives* – comes up with the second line of the song, followed by a credit for Dr Werner Kissling ('Directed and Photographed by . . .') and for the 'Editorial Supervision' of John Gifford.

Gifford was, in fact, the editor who was assisted by an unknown apprentice. The editing took place at Bush House in London (now the Headquarters of the BBC World Service) and, according to the un-named columnist 'Onlooker' in *Today's Cinema* in May 1935, it was Gifford who invited film correspondents and others who might be interested to see what was described as a 'version of Dr Kissling's Eriskay', and which the writer found '. . . unpretentious and naive – little effort, but a charm all of its own'.

The word 'version' is intriguing and tantalising. So is the date. Kissling had shot the film in 1934 and left Eriskay in September of that year. Did he cut his own version first and then, dissatisfied, or with an audience's dislike ringing in his ears, take it to a professional editor to make a better job of it? Even allowing for the première being held at the very end of April (and therefore Onlooker's mention of the film in the next and most relevant May issue of *Today's Cinema*), the final edit was clearly delayed until the late winter and early spring of 1935, some six to eight months after Kissling came back to London.

Dumfries Museum's collection of Kissling papers adds a further element to this speculation. In his papers there is another version of the film script – one

[1] The German *Bundesarkhiv* has expressed an interest in using its state-of-the-art technology to clean up the soundtrack and restore the film, but the new print now being made by the Scottish Film Archive may itself produce a significant improvement in sound quality.

that, whilst it echoes some of the lines of the final version, is much more academic in tone. This version, headed 'Eriskay, Film Commentary' (with a note in the top right-hand margin 'to be typed') consists of two handwritten and two roughly-typed pages, as well as a fair and better-typed copy of all four pages.

Kissling's original script (or what we have of it – the four pages are clearly not complete) is ethnologically based – examining the lifestyle of the 'Scottish Gael' and his or her crafts and occupations. It would make a good lecture, but a poor documentary.

Whatever happened, it appears (as with many films even today) that it required a good editor to mine the diamonds out of the mass of ore that Kissling had brought home. The next frame credits Duncan M. Morison for the 'Introductory Music' and the performer of the song we are still hearing – Sydney MacEwan.

The première was held at 9.30pm on April 30, 1935 in Londonderry House, home of the Marquis and Marchioness of Londonderry. Announced by poster and publication as 'A Hebridean Evening', the billing for the event is headed by the words 'Under the distinguished patronage of HRH The Prince of Wales, Lord of the Isles, who has graciously consented to be present if possible' and goes on to list other patrons including their Royal Highnesses the Duke and Duchess of York (with their subsidiary titles of Duke and Duchess of Inverness, presumably given in order to short up their local credentials for anything Hebridean), the Prime Minister, the Londonderry's themselves and a clutch of other notables including Cameron of Locheil, MacLeod of MacLeod and even Sir Godfrey Collins MP (whose connections to the Hebrides are not given and perhaps not even known!)

Of the artists taking part in the evening, it is Duncan Morison[2] who gets first billing, and although the film is prominently announced as a 'Preview . . . shortly to be released', Werner Kissling gets no mention at all.

Also performing were the London Gaelic Choir, and at the bottom of the poster there is an announcement that the 'entire net proceeds will be used to help the people of the Island of Eriskay to provide wool for spinning and weaving'.

Duncan Morison (spelt with one 'r' – not the usual way in the Western Isles) was known throughout his life as 'Major' – a *sloinneadh* or nickname that arose because his father's employer at Lews Castle was a Major Matheson. As a child Duncan used to spend much time at the castle, where the Major took a particular interest in him and because Duncan's middle name was Matheson, all the castle staff used to tease him by calling him 'The Major' too. No doubt the joke was more immediate at the time!

Equally unusual is Morison's story. As a youngster his musical talent drew much attention and he studied music in Glasgow and London where he

came to the attention of the Marchioness of Londonderry, a patron not just of the arts but of all things Hebridean. She used Morison as the mainstay of her 'Hebridean Evenings' which attracted the cream of London society. He composed, arranged and played for these and other events and kept a diary of his time in London, which his friend and fellow musician Mairead Hulse kindly discussed with him on tape in an effort to provide information for our documentary. Unfortunately that diary contains no references to Werner Kissling and in his old age he could remember little about the film, except the fact that he had played in a recording studio for it and that he did not get paid!

Island Moon was almost undoubtedly specially written as the opening music for the film. Its copyright date is 1935 but it sets to music a poem by another Western Isles' artist – Agnes Mure MacKenzie. The première's poster also credits Duncan Morison with 'collecting the songs . . . for this very beautiful record of island life' and it is therefore likely that Morison – who was deeply involved with the London Gaelic Choir – arranged for that body to sing them for Kissling and at the première. They performed often at Londonderry House in any case.

The singer would be equally familiar to the audience. The name of Sydney MacEwan is still well known to Scots over 60 as is the story of the Glasgow-born performer who in 1944 became a Catholic priest, serving in Glasgow, Lochgilphead, Rothesay and Kingussie and recorded sacred songs as Canon Sydney MacEwan for many years after the Second World War. He died in 1991, some three years after the man whose film he introduced at the age of 27.

I can remember, amongst boxes of old records under the upholstered window seat in my parent's front room in Troon, a particularly schmaltzy cover of a church in the snow and the same honeyed and curiously high voice of Sydney MacEwan performing Silent Night.

Sydney MacEwan must have sung Island Moon at the première as well as on the soundtrack, which the credits tell us was recorded at Imperial Sound Studios. During the making of the documentary Mairead Hulse provided a copy of the music but it was not possible to fit in a re-creation of its performance for our film. Had it been I would have asked Paul MacInnes of South Uist to sing it, as he did one memorable evening in my neighbour Archie McNaughton's house in Glendaruel, in Argyll. The words are somewhat overly romantic, but sung with a strong and rich Hebridean voice, it is a haunting piece of music.

The credits finish at the end of the first sentence of the second verse:
Low down in the west a waning moon calls to the sea
and as the next lines are sung:
Sweeping back the flood from the black points of land,
And the tide is turning from the seven rocks
a crawler runs up the screen introducing and placing the island of Eriskay.

---

[2] Duncan was still alive in Stornoway in 1995 when our documentary was made.

This narrative continues throughout the whole of verse five (in the song verses three and four are not sung, but are given in the published sheet music) and only when it is over do we see, fading out of the black, a close-up of the side and rigging of a boat, the sea and the shore of Eriskay.

This narrative does not feature in Kissling's first script. Its language is flowery and obviously designed to draw in those who view the Hebrides through tartan-tinted spectacles. I suspect its presence owes much to the advice of John Gifford who would have seen that it was necessary to 'place' the film for its audience and to ring some familiar bells before any detail was given.

This is what the crawler on the screen says:

Distant some sixty-odd miles from the West Coast of Scotland lie the outer Hebrides. ISLES OF ENCHANTMENT rich in legend and famed for their songs of surpassing beauty. Shrouded in the wind-driven mists of the restless Atlantic or glowing strangely in a shaft of evening light beyond the jagged outlines of the Coolins of Skye their remoteness enthrals. Yet their rocky coastline, the ultimate buttress against the Western Ocean and resounding only to the ever present murmur of mighty waters or the shrill cries of innumerable gulls, harbours a race whose history is rooted in the first glimmerings of a remote past and whose traditions are borne upon numberless songs and airs famous wherever Gael meets Gael the world over.

We must not forget that whilst today most audiences would have only the sketchiest idea where Eriskay was, to an audience before the war – and particularly to an older audience – the songs of Margaret Kennedy Fraser would still be familiar and the Eriskay Love Lilt, in particular, would have been sung in most school music classes.

And although political correctness may have changed the way in which we speak of, or introduce, faraway places, the lush style of the introduction to Kissling's film is no different from a thousand travelogues of the first half of this century. Even its random capital letters and paucity in punctuation speak of breathless artificial excitement.

I like to think that Kissling fought long and hard against such an introduction to a place and a people he had come to know and respect, but I suspect not. Whilst the style is not his, (the opening of his first script runs prosaically: 'Eriskay is one of the smaller inhabited islands in the long chain of the broken Hebrides.') he did from time to time exhibit a romantic view of the island and the islanders. At a later date this was usually to the fore in his letters to the Scottish office about the need to improve the water supply, or introduce handloom weaving (a cause dear to his heart) but, one suspects, of not much interest to those he was condemning to a boring and back-breaking life at the loom.

English was also Kissling's second (perhaps third) language. Absolutely fluent as he was, the convoluted alliterations and elaborate copywriting of the crawler were not , I think, within his stylistic range and it is most likely that they are the work of some other hand who persuaded him (if persuasion was needed) that this method of attack would have the most success.

It is an attack that is complimented by the words of verse five of Island Moon, which play as the crawler rises up the screen:
Perhaps the moon is shining for you in the far country?
But the skies there are not Island skies!
You will remember the salt smell of the sea and the little rain.
goes the song, conjuring up distance and exile and the longing for 'the island' – as most island dwellers call their home, no matter which one they belong to.

Romantic and seemingly over-emotional as this is, it does equate (perhaps even accidentally) with true feeling. I know that my wife from North Uist, can feel the call of her island at particular times, and I (a mere incomer) have felt something stir as the ferry sets sail from Skye to what is only, at that stage, a long dark line on the horizon.

An elderly, very distinguished and senior local authority official told me one night over a dram in South Uist that he had once felt that call so intensely – and so visibly – that he had deserted a teaching job near Glasgow in order to be where the salmon were rising. In his story he had actually seen the back wall of a classroom in the inner-city schoolroom change to a rushing stream on the second-last day of the summer term in June, and there and then he had left the school and set off for home, so strong was the call.

Gael and Gall would be affected by the music, if not by the words, and this introduction to the film – whoever devised it, and no matter how dated – is undoubtedly moving.

The opening shot of the film is, however, pure Kissling. No one else could be responsible for the atmospheric shot of the sea, the boat and the coast. We see it now in a faded form, but in the original print the grey quality of the sky, the hills and the sea must have contrasted beautifully with the black shadow of the boat deck, and indeed with the black screen into which the image fades. The playing with light and shape is very typical of Kissling as a photographer and the shot (with the sound of the creaking of the boat spars and the cry of seagulls, added during edit) is tremendously atmospheric. It takes an audience out of their comfortable seats (the gilded chairs of Londonderry house to start with) and into the wild Western Isles. But it takes them there in some style!

After an intervening and slightly wider shot of the boat and the shore, the scene changes to a wide shot of the yacht and (more prominently) the west coast of the island of Eriskay. This shot coincides with the opening of the commentary.

Everything before the commentary starts is an introduction to Kissling's film and this preamble was, I feel sure, foisted on Kissling by an editor, yet it does open up the audience for the stunning detail that Kissling has observed and recorded. It conjures up the spirit of the place and creates a tangible feeling for the island that Kissling himself had come to know well.

A STILL FROM THE SEQUENCE INVOLVING THE ENTANGLED SHEEP.

CHAPTER 4

A Viewing of the Film

The film proper begins with the spoken commentary – and the commentary here is Kissling's – at least after the first flowery sentence. It moves quickly into the anthropological description of the 'crofter/fishermen' and cuts again within a few seconds, after our first sight of an Eriskay pony (the small, hardy breed unique to the island) to people: a man and woman cutting corn with a sickle.

The cutting of corn in the Western Isles takes place later than on the mainland, so it is likely that these shots were taken well into Kissling's visit to the island – probably in late July or early August. The corn appears to be relatively undamaged, indicating a reasonable summer, and the next shot – of a hillside with Kissling's yacht coming round a headland – shows 'lazybeds' with a full growth of potatoes, again probably taken in August.

This opening of the film is what one might call the 'arrival' sequence. It intercuts shots of the yacht approaching and entering the harbour at Eriskay[1]. Although the harbour is on the eastern side of the island, the first shot is of the boat on the western side, so in effect Kissling has created a 'cheat' – film being the only industry in which that word is quite respectable. Shots of the harvesting and, later on, one or two of the black houses and the older inhabitants of the island follow. It also features close-ups of the yacht taken on the vessel itself and – mixed over the bird calls – the creaking of the boat timbers and the first song from the London Gaelic choir; some navigation instructions from an individual on the yacht whose face is just out

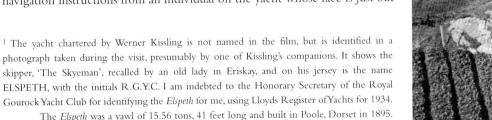

[1] The yacht chartered by Werner Kissling is not named in the film, but is identified in a photograph taken during the visit, presumably by one of Kissling's companions. It shows the skipper, 'The Skyeman', recalled by an old lady in Eriskay, and on his jersey is the name ELSPETH, with the initials R.G.Y.C. I am indebted to the Honorary Secretary of the Royal Gourock Yacht Club for identifying the *Elspeth* for me, using Lloyds Register of Yachts for 1934.

The *Elspeth* was a yawl of 15.56 tons, 41 feet long and built in Poole, Dorset in 1895. In addition to her sails she was equipped with a two-cylinder petrol motor and was owned by the brothers John and William Adam. Registered originally to Falmouth as her home port, by 1934 she was based at the Cove Yard in Gourock. There is no record of her being broken up, but it is unlikely she has survived to see a century.

of shot, and then, when the shot widens, is too indistinct to recognise.

This individual is dressed in what might be called classic Western Isles sailing gear: a jersey, which might be an 'Eriskay' – the distinct type of pullover with traditional patterns crafted by the women of the island – and boots and dark trousers. It is tempting to think that it might be Kissling himself and because the voice is clearly post-dubbed and almost artificially English, this is a possibility.

The question of the recording of the film sound is one that occurs again and again during the film's duration of 19 minutes. In addition to his 35mm camera, Kissling had sound recording equipment with him on Eriskay, but the quality of the soundtrack is such that it is obvious that the sound was post-dubbed – using his own in situ recordings and other recordings made later in a studio. Certainly the music is post-dubbed, as we have seen from the memories of Major Duncan Morison.

The next intercut shot is one of children, ostensibly watching the yacht, although almost undoubtedly 'cheated' with later material. Walking away from the camera is another Eriskay pony, this one loaded with the two panniers that in later shots we see are used to carry peat home.

I have an original photograph by Kissling in front of me as I write – it shows two ponies with these panniers, accompanied by two children, identified as Allan Johnstone and one of the MacInnes girls (see below). One of the sets of panniers is full of peat, and the other contains what looks like the utensils for a picnic, much needed on a day spent doing the back-breaking work of heaving and loading peats.

On the back of the photo is a hand-written dedication: *Rosalind and Andrew with love from Werner* and it is readily identifiable as having been penned very late in his life. Underneath the dedication is a title for the photograph: *Pladh in position, Eriskay 1953.*

Dwelly's definitive Gaelic dictionary defines *Pladhach* as being the same as *Platach* which is a Wester Ross Gaelic term for a mat of plaited straw, put on a horse's back under the saddle. 'Plat' can mean any heavy covering and it may be that Kissling has written the word down when told it without regard to the Eriskay accent and the Gaelic similarity in pronunciation between 't' and 'd'.

Children feature again and again in Kissling's photographs and in his film. David Lockwood, Kissling's executor, has a wonderful enlargement of one of Kissling's photographs of children in a prominent place in his house – it is a photograph of children on a boat, and is full of character and enquiry (see page 99). Kissling is also well and kindly remembered in South Uist by those who knew him when they were children. He seems to have had an easy and friendly manner with young people and to have had his fondness for them reciprocated.

We switch back to the boat, and to the close-up of an old man (who features in some of the still photographs taken in Eriskay in 1934) before a wide shot of a traditional black house (probably at Acairseid, where the harbour was and still is). This is followed by a close-up of smoke coming from the window of such a house and then by two more exterior views before we see the old couple outside the building.

The commentary proper has started at this stage. In keeping with the romantic, quaint and historic tone set by the 'crawler' at the start of the film, the first words are about the 1745 Jacobite Rising and a supposedly fresh memory of that event and of Charles Edward Stuart in the minds of present-day islanders. But the words are intended also to create an image of the island as unchanged and unspoilt: *A house just such as this as made him welcome, and just such a scene as this as met his eyes for little has changed in this corner of Gaeldom.*

This sentence runs on over shots of two more black houses and then the background song covers shots of the track over to the harbour and a wide

shot of an island bay, with a small boat in it.

I am indebted to Alasdair MacAskill, my wife's uncle, for his patience and help when we looked at the film again and again and tried to identify all the songs in the film. We failed with three, largely because of the poor quality of the soundtrack, but did manage to be reasonably certain of several others – including the one I have just mentioned which is *Morag Bheag nean Mhurachaidh an t-saoir.*

The scene then changes to people on the track, and a solo Gaelic song. Immediately we see two island children – the younger not more than two or three years old – walking barefoot along the track, and the picture cuts back to the longer shot, with adults and a chicken running across, close to the camera.

There is then a high shot of a woman leading an Eriskay pony, with two laden creels on its back, both full of peat. This gathering of peat from the banks is a task for the mid-summer, so again we can date the shot to late July or early August, unless it was a particularly fine year when the peats would have dried more quickly.

This shot continues until the pony is at a house, at which time Kissling cuts to the peats being unloaded and thrown on the ground prior to stacking. There is already part of stack built, but given the speed at which peat burns (and the fact that it was the only winter fuel) a large stack would be required for each household, and the task of loading and bringing the peats home by pony pannier would have been a long one.

This sequence brings to an end the second Gaelic Song – *Mo Grhaide trom is duilich leum* – and ushers in the third, this time with a male voice – *Leannan Mo Ghaoil Mairi Bhan.*

The male voice is appropriate enough, because the shots are now of two boys with the pony, and the camera follows the boys up the hillside to the peat bank itself, where the peat is loaded into the panniers. The shot

clearly identifies the hillside, with a view westwards to Barra on the horizon – it is the north-west slope of Ben Scrien.

The camera then pans round the hillside to the peat cuttings before following one of the boys on the downward journey, with the sands of Prince's Strand clearly behind him. But the next cut shifts the scene (it is almost a repeat shot of the earlier pan across the bay with the small boat seen in the middle of the water), in order to establish a change of subject. After a brief move right from the shot, the picture changes to the stacking of corn, with the song now almost faded away.

The couple who had been cutting corn are now stacking it, but the actions don't appear to be contiguous. The corn crop now looks as if there has been some rain or wind damage, and the stacking may be repairs to previous stacks. The shot moves to the woman undertaking the same task, briefly back to the elderly man for the start of a new section of commentary, and then back to the woman completing the task.

A primitive life may be . . . starts the text, to the call of seabirds (mostly oyster-catchers which have been used several times in the soundtrack and which were probably recorded by Kissling on location) and then goes on:

. . . one with the cry of seabirds and the roar of breaking waters ever in the ear. A race of men less tenacious than these would long ago have given up the struggle. Nurtured under such hard conditions they are content with what they hold and are happy to work the often meagre soil or face the dangers of tempestuous seas.

The voice-over continues after the woman with a wide shot of sheep in a rocky and hilly landscape, and then cuts to a striking shot of sheep on a hillside above the camera, the animals silhouetted against the sky as they run downhill. The film returns to the open wide shot and this is held longer than it merits, while the commentary ends. There is a pause, and then the sounds of the sheep bleating occurs just before a cut looking down on sheep being

gathered in a rocky hollow.

These shots are the start to the longest sequence of the film – a sequence devoted to sheep and the uses to which their wool is put. After the shot of the gathering and a man chasing and directing the sheep, there is a lengthy shot of sheep in the hollow, with two rams butting each other at the edge of the composition. Although this should be the focus of the scene, it is curiously offset, as if Kissling himself did not see it when looking through the viewfinder and it has only found its way into the final edit when the activity of the rams became apparent.

When the scene changes to a closer shot of the sheep, the next part of the commentary starts.

Their security lies in wool for upon this uncharitable soil sheep thrive and make possible the home industry of weaving the enduring cloth well known to all.

Whilst these words are being narrated the first shot of sheep is slow-mixed to a second shot; the first time a mix has been used instead of a cut. The effect is of a river of sheep moving from left to right, although the intrusion of a head and shoulders (and shepherd's crook) in the bottom of the frame adds a slightly distracting element to the move.

The soundtrack again cuts to bleating sheep whilst the pictures move on to show local men penning them and then sitting on the fank wall. The men appear to be wearing traditional Eriskay jerseys, and they all hold sticks to help them gather even the youngest of the flock.

There is now a brief cut to a woman walking towards the fank, holding what looks like a skien of discarded wool, and then cuts equally briefly to a man in the fank and then back to the woman whilst in the background there is some indistinct Gaelic conversation, owing to the damaged soundtrack.[2]

Kissling now returns to the rams butting each other. In a delightful sequence of 14 separate shots during which the rams get their horns tangled, an attempt is made by one man to split them apart but he fails and then calls on another for help. Then whilst two dogs run around them, the men set to their task and eventually one of them has to turn one of the rams upside down to disengage the horns and finally free them.

This whole sequence is relayed with a liberal use of cutaways of sheep, of the woman who has arrived at the fank, and of a group of men, again shot from below their seat on the wall, from which they gesture with their sticks. Thirty five seconds in length, it is a finely observed miniature story, which shows either the work of a highly experienced editor, or the planning of a good director – and perhaps a bit of both.

What appeared to be the skein of wool in the woman's hands is now shown to a be a tether of some sort, and the film now moves to the dipping and shearing of the sheep. A line of men pass the sheep out of the fank and into a dipping trough, from which they are placed in a wooden run, to be checked off before being released. There is clearly some joke going on, with the men at times amused either by the proximity of the camera, or more likely by the humour that often accompanies a community working together in this way. On the second track the conversation continues, and draws towards a close with a clear *'Tha mi falabh'*.[3] Meanwhile the soaking sheep run off in

[2] It is to be hoped that the repairs and a new print will allow a complete transcript at last and the chance to determine whether the snatches of Gaelic conversation are artificial – probably contributed by members of the London Gaelic Choir and recorded in studio for post-dubbing – or are, as I think they may be, fragments from actual recordings made by Kissling on Eriskay in 1934.

[3] 'I am going'.

close-up, going past another carved shepherd's crook, which this time is stuck firmly in the ground while its owner works at the dipping.

The scene then suddenly changes to the hill above Haun, with South Uist clearly visible across the Sound of Eriskay. This is followed by a close-up of the clipping that is now taking place, with a very placid sheep being trimmed with rather small-looking shears. The conversation on the soundtrack is now that of women's voices.

The use of wide shots of the sea and landscape appear to be a device designed to allow a change of subject or pace. Obviously clipping does not follow on from dipping exactly in this way, but the narrative flow (such as it is) is punctuated by the landscapes in order to make just that point.

It is a woman who is doing the clipping, and as she gathers the wool together, the scene changes to a different grey-haired woman who has been soaking the fleece. Another landscape shot intervenes, of corn or hay waving in the wind, and then the film cuts back to the woman who stands and looks ahead of her – at which point there is another cut, supposedly giving her viewpoint and showing the bare hillside, up which she and a companion walk with a metal cauldron full of wool between them, which they lay out on a rock to dry.

The soundtrack at this point mixes both song and conversation with women's voices – and immediately the pictures cut to the outside of a black house with a man walking towards it from the right. This initial shot gives way to yet another woman teasing out the dried wool by hand, as she moves slowly towards a spinning wheel, situated outside the front door.

There is now a brief cutaway (presumably to the woman's husband) who is mending fishing line outside the house (this coincides with a man's voice on the indistinguishable soundtrack) and then the scene shifts again to

a woman kneeling on rocks, gathering a substance from the surfaces around her.

The commentary (which has been silent for several minutes) starts again at this point.

The dyes are natural and are scraped from the rocks: this is known as crotal or lichen as it is called elsewhere . . .

There is another slow mix here, which lends a somewhat ghostly appearance to the woman, whose face cannot be seen – this may be deliberate in view of what is to follow.

. . . and gives a rich brown colour to the cloth, but all sorts of vegetables and flowers are used for other colours. Their respect for the common rights for this very necessary commodity is such that around the flickering light of the will o' the wisp, which may be seen sometimes at nightfall over the bogs, a legend has arisen. There was a man, a blacksmith by trade, who went out at night unknown to his comrades to scrape a little crotal. The devil cursed him and the community knew him no more. He was turned away into outer darkness, forever banished to wander through the dark nights searching for crotal. The devil gave him one consolation and that was that he might take an ember of his fire to help him in his search.'

This traditional story is told in different ways, about different commodities, in different places, but certainly a range of distinct colours for wool and for cloth was much prized in the days before artificial dyes, and even today those who experiment with natural dyes are often guarded about what they use and where they get it.[4]

---

[4] There is a Uist story about a much-prized blue colour of wool which was complimented upon by a distinguished English visitor who enquired of the woman of the house how she obtained the hue. 'That', she says, 'is from my John's pisspot', and because urine was used for fulling the cloth, it is a believable story, although one that may have diminished the demand for her wool for quite a while!

The story of the blacksmith is told in a sequence of pictures that moves from the scraping of the rock, to another cutaway of the man mending his fishing line and then to the preparation of the wool with the crotal over an open, outdoor, peat fire (with the sheepdog wandering around in the background for authenticity's sake, no doubt!)

The shots alternate between the preparation of the wool and the preparation of the fishing line (with the soundtrack alternating too between the Gaelic women's voices and another song) until a sudden cut to a local fishing boat in virtually full frame – her masts still canted down as she sets out to sea. She is most probably a line drifter, and as she leaves the harbour she is passed on the far side by a boat returning, masts up.

There are clearly three men on board the boat, but as soon as the shot is established we cut again to the wool dying, before returning to another boat – this time in full close-up, with her registration mark (CY.425) clearly visible. The CY mark is for Castlebay, Barra, which would have been the nearest registration port.

The sound of the vessel's steam engine is clear on the soundtrack but because it is so clear it must have been added in studio. What is not artificial, though, are the piles of buoys and fishing line on her deck. The face of the crewman who emerges from the engine-room is also startlingly sharp as he is caught by the morning light looking across to the camera which was probably on Kissling's yacht.

As the boat moves out of shot, the film cuts back again to wool, this time to the removal of the dyed wool from the pot on the outdoor fire. The soundtrack has again gone from women's to men's voices as the subject goes from wool to fishing and back again, and no sooner have we watched the wool being removed (with a metal spoon) then we cut back yet again to the

fishing, and to two men on the prow of a boat, shot from the boat itself. But that shot is over almost instantaneously, and we return to the wool and another song.

As the wool is taken from its bowl and carried over to be dried on the walls of the house, the commentary starts again: *With the drying of the wool, the old spinning wheel that has done service from generation to generation now plays its part. And how many beautiful songs have been made at such wheels as these, it would be hard to say.*

The spinning wheel is now at work, and alongside the spinner another woman cards the wool, using traditional carding combs, passing the carded wool for spinning. The soundtrack is more distinct here than elsewhere, and clearly (in Gaelic) the spinner is offering to make a cup of tea. Then, as the shots intersperse between spinning and carding, another song starts – this time *Mac An Airidh.*

As a white hen walks out of the house, the commentary continues: *There is something possibly in the turning wheel and the 'thud, thud' of the foot that drives it, that calls for song. Or something in the twisting thread maybe that lends inspiration to the spinner.*

There is a pause for a number of quite detailed cutaways of the spinning and carding, and then the voice resumes to a full shot of the turning wheel: *Music is in the soul of these people and it is as natural as talk. There are songs of weaving, songs of spinning, songs for carding, songs for the crotal gathering. Traditional and melodious as only such a people could make, living as they do in a land where the errant voices of the wind forever whisper. But of all their songs there are none more spirited, or which call for more united effort of harmony and rhythm, than when the cloth is waulked or beaten till the fibres swell and the cloth is fully shrunk. It may take ten songs to make it so, for here is a people who reckon effort, nay even life itself, by*

the length of a song: a people with a lesson for us all and who are able to transmute the dross of individual drudgery to the gold of united effort by the power of melody.

This paen of praise to the effects of Gaelic song is accompanied by shots of spun wool being gathered into balls by using a revolving spindle – of different balls of wool being laid out for weaving, and of a *luadh*, or waulking of the cloth.

There are three luadhs on film that I know of – one reconstructed for the School of Scottish Studies in the sixties, complete with a box of washing powder accidentally left on the table; one for a 1940s' short fiction film about a missing sailor who is washed up on his home island, and this one. But Kissling's one is the most original, with the large wooden tub in which the tweed has been 'fulled' or shrunk (usually at that time in urine), and the solid board on which the material is turned and pounded again and again until it is finished.

This luadh is not only authentic – it is actuality, complete with the old potato sacks on which the women sit. And although the waulking song is clearly recorded and post-dubbed (the women of the London Gaelic Choir, almost certainly perform this) the energy of the event shines clearly through.

The songs that Kissling heard – and which he would not have understood – would have been much livelier in content than the parlour version in the film, but waulking songs were often scatological and concerned with the shortcomings of the men of the community . . . and of any visitors who happened to be around!

One of the shots in the middle of the luadh is, almost unconsciously, an image of tremendous contrasts. The younger women are working with enthusiasm, but at the end of the table, standing against the sky, is an older women. She is wearing the traditional clothes of the island, with the dark headscarf, but the younger women are bare-armed and wear modern floral-pattern dresses. This shot alone speaks volumes of what is happening right in front of Kissling himself – as he records the past, the present is rushing in.

At the conclusion of the luadh the cloth is rolled and folded, with great precision and then beaten again. And this time the old women and the younger women all take part.

The shot changes abruptly to evening and fishing boats coming home. Then there is a close-up of a man in the bows of a boat against the sky, and this coincides with a reprise of the opening song:
Who will not remember the salt smell of the sea and the little rain.

The picture cuts quickly to the sheep being gathered and then to an open shot of the sea and the sky from the east side of the island. And as that shot fades to black, the words,
THE END
fade up in white.

Many of those who know the film have thought that the ending is unduly truncated, and, as I pointed out in chapter three, Janet McBain has often wondered if perhaps there was not a longer version which has somehow got lost. But I now think the flow of the commentary, and particularly the final section which seems to summarise Kissling's view of the virtues of the people of Eriskay, indicate that the film is coming to an end at that stage.

And in any case there is, the more one watches it, a clear internal structure, if not a clear enough narrative line. The film starts with a 'placing' of the island and some sketchy information on its most famous moment in history – the landing of Charles Edward Stuart in 1744. It then briefly looks at agriculture and peat-cutting and by way of explanation of the poor soil leads into an examination of the 'sheep-based' industries that the people are involved in, with some sideways glances at fishing as an occupation. It concludes by tying together the domestic life of the people with their culture and concludes on the note of romanticism with which it began.

As an essay, or adjunct, or illustration for Kissling's studies it would surely act as a powerful *aide-mémoire*, as well as informing and entertaining those who know virtually nothing about the Western Isles and her people. And the lack of artifice, its placing of so little between the lens and the viewer, give it, almost by accident, a tremendous power – with the odd flicker of amazement each time it is seen: a flicker caused by the sharp profile of a face, or the clear and direct look of a person probably long-dead, straight into the camera and into our lives today.

But they were not seeing us, or their future audiences. They were seeing an unknown, elegant, wealthy enquirer, from a faraway country and of whom they knew virtually nothing.

Who, indeed, was Werner Kissling?

THE FIRST PICTURE OF WERNER KISSLING. HE RECALLED
BEING IN A 'BAD MOOD, BUT MY MOTHER CHARMED ME
OUT OF IT'

CHAPTER 5

Pictures of a Childhood

Werner Kissling was born into some considerable wealth – if not the highest social position – on April 11, 1895 in the family home, Heizendorf, near Breslau in Silesia, the second of three sons to Georg and Johanna Kissling. His father was the third generation of a Silesian brewing family whose origins lay further west. Having settled near Breslau in Silesia, Werner's great-grandfather did well, and his grandfather and father fared even better. By the time Werner was born the family home was a substantial 18th-century schloss decorated like a wedding cake, which dominated the family estate. Amongst the papers that Kissling left there are several pictures of the house including one which looks as if it has been taken in winter with the lake 'frozen' and the place looking like a set for *Mayerling*; the illusion having been created by the length of exposure of the shot. There are also two pictures of the interior taken during his childhood which portray huge formal rooms with heavy drapes and French furniture.

Kissling's upbringing was that of a 19th-century German aristocrat. His family had achieved with wealth what others had achieved only by birth, and late 19th-century Silesia was the heartland of the German propertied barons. It was composed of huge estates, and – despite the recent memory of the Kulturkampf[1] – was something of a centre of Catholic reaction where power, privilege and breeding counted for nearly everything. Another of his personal photographs shows his mother and father in formal pose, staring straight at the camera with an arrogance betraying money and power. A companion shot shows Georg Kissling with his three sons, the inevitable sailor suits adorning them (see page 27).

Photographs – which were to become the constant companion of Kissling's life – were much in evidence in his childhood too. He retained a number from that time, including one of his mother and father in India, on one of their regular tours abroad. Another of these took place when Kissling was 10 – probably in the late summer. One record of it was kept by Kissling amongst his personal papers until he died – a postcard from the Western Isles in his mother's handwriting sending love to Werner and his brother. This tour by Werner's mother would not have been an uncommon trip even at that time for wealthy Germans. They would have travelled in style to London, by fast rail-sleeper to Glasgow or even Fort William and continued on a steamship tour of the West Coast of Scotland and the Western Isles.

We have a later record of such a trip – another film in the Scottish Film Archive, known as the 'St Kilda 1923' film. This was the ultimate destination of all such trips. The most remote place in the British Isles, the small group of islands known in English as St Kilda, although no such name exists in Gaelic. All the islands have separate names in that language, the largest (and only inhabited one) being called Hirta.

This is one of only three extant films of Hirta when it was inhabited. One of them simply records the evacuation and was kept hidden until the late 1970s because it was made by a crew member on the evacuation ship, SS *Dunera Castle*, against the strict regulations which surrounded the evacuation procedure. Newsmen and cameras were prohibited. The 'St Kilda 1923' film was taken by an anonymous cameraman on board a steamer that called at Oban, Dunvegan on Skye, at other ports in the Western Isles and ultimately at Hirta where the local inhabitants appear less than pleased to see tourists and – in one sequence – appear to throw stones at the cameraman.

In 1905 the tourist trips to Hirta would have been somewhat better received – provided they did not call on the Sabbath, for the island at that time was in the grip of a fierce and exclusive Sabbatarianism which prohibited any work on a Sunday, including the unloading of vital supplies from ships that might only have one day of good weather to offload their essential cargoes for the winter.

[1] The 'Conflict of Beliefs'. This was a term used to apply to the dispute between Bismarck and the Roman Catholic Church (1871-87). Bismarck feared that the Catholic Church was asserting a prior claim to the state on the obedience of its members and laws forbade priests to mention politics in their sermons. The Jesuits were also expelled. Many priests chose imprisonment rather than acceptance of the laws and Bismarck, realising the sympathetic response of the public to those being persecuted, negotiated a settlement of the dispute with Pope Leo XIII which resulted in most Catholic rights being restored.

WINTER AT HEIZENDORF – TAKEN DURING WERNER KISSLING'S
CHILDHOOD, PROBABLY BY HIS MOTHER.

THE DRAWING ROOM AT HEIZENDORF TAKEN AT ROUGHLY THE SAME TIME.

St Kilda in the early 20th century was dependent upon tourism to a greater extent than any of the other islands and Kissling's mother would certainly have been inveigled into buying tweed or something stuffed with the feathers of seabirds. She would also have 'sent' a card from the village post office, and carried it away herself with the unique postmark on it. She also took a number of photographs.

In 1995 I was approached by Calum Fergusson, another Gaelic film-maker, who had heard a rumour that Kissling had taken photographs in St Kilda. Whilst Kissling most probably did visit St Kilda in 1934, probably on the way back from Eriskay in his yacht, there are no photographs or films which he took in any of the collections to support this notion. But some months later, when reviewing the glass slides he left in two wooden boxes (which his executor and friend David Lockwood still has) I found two photographs that are undoubtedly taken on St Kilda – both of which include some of the inhabitants as we know them from photographs taken by a number of others. These photographs seem to have been taken by Kissling's mother, and can, most probably, be dated to her visit.

Johanna Kissling was an extraordinary woman. Strong-willed, she accepted the discipline of Werner's childhood home whilst developing a particular closeness to her second son. The first photograph we have of Werner is with his mother. Aged less than a year, he later recalled having been told that he was 'in a bad mood' when the photograph was taken but that his mother had, 'as usual, charmed me out of it'.

The Kissling family was not particularly close. Werner's memories of his father were not warm, and with a succession of governesses and a range of staff, his parents must have been distant and any contact with them was formal. Werner, like his brothers, was educated at home for the first seven years of his life (the governess no doubt being either French or English) but in 1902 he started to attend the Gymnasium of St Mary Magdalene in Breslau and later moved to the gymnasium in Leobschutz. These schools were run along disciplined lines, with the expectation that the young men who attended would finish their education in both the army and at a university. The class system was much in evidence, and the responsibilities that rested on the shoulders of the privileged were also strongly emphasised.

In the first part of the 20th century Silesia was undoubtedly provincial, but within living memory those who lived there experienced the transformation of their country. In the 30 years preceding Werner's birth Germany had fought three wars and had been united as the German Empire in 1871.[2]

In 1890 Bismarck resigned as Chancellor (giving rise to the famous 'Dropping the Pilot' cartoon in *Punch*) and as the young Werner was growing

[2] In the Franco-Prussian War of 1870, Werner's grandfather, Conrad August Carl Kissling, had served as a 28-year-old volunteer officer.

GEORG AND JOHANNA KISSLING, APRIL 1899 WHEN WERNER WAS FOUR. THE PICTURE WAS TAKEN IN A BERLIN STUDIO.

THE INEVITABLE 'SAILOR SUIT' PORTRAIT. GUNTHER, GEORG, WERNER AND GEORG CONRAD IN THE EARLY YEARS OF THIS CENTURY

GEORG AND JOHANNA KISSLING VISITING INDIA, AROUND 1900

up, the militaristic, Pan-German enthusiasm which had sidelined Bismarck was reaching its zenith. Werner's education would have included Latin, German literature, mathematics, a good helping of German history and some form of military training. Uniforms were a part of his growing up – he kept pictures of himself in a variety of uniforms and even the earliest pictures have him dressed up in rather militaristic clothes: the 'sailor suit' which I have already mentioned, a form of clothing still beloved of parents half-a-century later, but fortunately nowhere to be seen today.

Military concerns dominated his society and at the level in which his family circulated, such concerns would have had a direct impact. The economy was gearing up for war and the business establishment supported and encouraged such developments. Clearly the family wealth continued to increase in the first decade of the 20th century. Johanna was able to indulge her interests in photography and in expensive travel: and the brewery businesses were able to finance the grand style in which they lived. The castle at Heizendorf was added to and developed and the family were well able to afford the staff needed to maintain their privileged lifestyle.

In the summer Werner learned to sail on the lake beside the castle: in winter, wrapped in furs and warm boots, he skated on it. The Kissling's entertained in the manner that became them: Kissling's nephew remembers stories of grand parties, with the entrance hall of Heizendorf (the oldest part of the building) alive with guests who received their first drink of the evening at the foot of the staircase, before moving on into the ballroom and the salons. Werner's childhood would not have been dissimilar (excepting the elitism of public schooling) to that of his contemporaries in Scotland at that time. The nearest parallel would have been great brewing and distilling families like the Youngers, the Ushers and the Buchanans who built grand houses, entertained royally and worked themselves into the structure and fabric of the Establishment. And with less prejudice about 'trade' and the money it produced, in Silesia the Kissling's would have moved in the highest echelons of society. By 1910, that society became more and more convinced that war was inevitable.

The Kruger Telegram, the Moroccan Crisis and the Agadir Incident had contributed to a process of armament by Britain, France and Germany and with the laying down of Germany's first dreadnought in 1907 the final race to be prepared for the inevitable hostilities was underway. Werner Kissling was coming to the end of his schooldays in June 1914 when a pistol shot in Sarajevo precipitated another international crisis. Six weeks later Germany was at war with Britain and France and Werner Kissling was preparing to join the army.

WERNER KISSLING IN THE UNIFORM OF THE PRUSSIAN
GUARD, WHICH HE JOINED IN SEPTEMBER 1914.

CHAPTER 6

Soldier and Diplomat

In August 1914 Werner Kissling joined one of the elite German regiments – the Prussian Guard. One of Werner's oldest friends, the explorer Andrew Croft, of whom we will hear more later, retains a photograph of Werner in his uniform taken shortly after he joined. Amongst Werner's suitcase of photographs and papers is another such photograph, in a leather display case that contains four separate shots – Kissling and his two brothers and father, all in uniform, and all apparently taken in the opening month of 1915. Just months later his younger brother Gunther was dead – killed in Russia on September 25, 1915, at the age of 19 years and three months.

Gunther was brought home to be buried in the family graveyard on a tongue of land jutting into the lake near the house. There is a simple plate inscribed to him, but above it stands a massive stone monument engraved with the fatalistic sentiment that might stand as an epitaph for a whole lost generation: *Everything comes from God, happiness and unhappiness, life and death.*

Next to him lies his father Georg Kissling who survived the war for only a short time, dying at the comparatively young age of 55 in 1922.

Werner, as a member of the elite of the German army, was quickly aware of the awful slaughter that was taking place. Within a few months more than half of those who had joined up with him were dead. But he determined to do something to increase his chances of living beyond the war. At the end of 1914 he volunteered for the German Navy and although inter-service transfers were unusual, he was accepted and served for the remaining four years somewhere on the German coast.

His fascination for sailing may have been engendered by lazy summer days at Heizendorf where the lake was large enough to take small boats and – in the ordered manner of his upbringing – probably had facilities for

FATHER AND SONS – FIRST WORLD WAR PORTRAITS. THE SONS ARE SECOND LEFT TO RIGHT: GEORG CONRAD, WERNER AND GUNTHER.
THESE ARE THE PICTURES WERNER KEPT IN A LEATHER DISPLAY CASE FOR THE REST OF HIS LIFE.

GUNTHER'S MAKESHIFT GRAVE ON THE RUSSIAN FRONT, 1915. HE WAS
REBURIED AT HEIZENDORF SOMETIME IN 1916.

THE FAMILY GRAVEYARD AT HEIZENDORF, SHOWING THE GRAVES OF
GUNTHER AND HIS FATHER.

learning to sail properly. It was a skill he was to use again when he came to the Western Isles 20 years later.

Just as the First World War changed English society utterly and swept away the grace and languor of the Edwardian era, so the events of 1914-18 changed the future for wealthy German families like the Kisslings.

These changes were perhaps slow to dawn on Johanna, left at home at Heizendorf. Breslau was distant from either of the war fronts and after the peace with Russia in 1917, Silesia was no longer even on the route to war. With none of the total war techniques that were to be used on the continent within the next 30 years, it was possible for Johanna and her friends to maintain their lifestyle in much the same manner to which they had become accustomed since the end of the last century.

Yet although the brewery and the family lands continued to earn money, the family was disrupted and to some extent destroyed. Gunther was sorely missed and both Werner and his elder brother Georg Conrad served throughout the war in their different services. Their experiences – and the bitter experience of defeat and the imposition of the Versailles Treaty – made them less secure, less cosmopolitan and more aware of the difficulties on the continent. Some of those were comparatively close to home. Poland, which had virtually ceased to exist in the 19th century, was re-created as an independent nation in 1919. Silesia was now on the borders of Germany and there was a sense of insecurity created just by that change.

The surrender of Germany in November 1918, the exile of the Kaiser and the confusion of the next three years took its toll on Werner. Whilst remaining in the navy until the spring of 1919 he would have witnessed the civil unrest that resulted in the Spartacist revolt and the near slide of Germany into communism, as well as the actions of some of his fellow officers in resisting the political turmoil – resistance that led to the murder of Rosa Luxemburg and Karl Leibnicht in January 1919. The officers involved in Luxemburg's murder were the officer corps of the Weimar Republic and it was in the service of that republic that Werner now started to undergo training. His first post was obtained in July 1919 as a member of the diplomatic staff posted to Riga in what was to eventually become Latvia.

The first photographs in our possession taken by Werner Kissling date from this posting to Riga. These, however, do not show the beauties of the old city or the river, but instead are photographs of tanks, artillery and helmeted soldiers.

In 1919 the three Baltic states of Estonia, Lithuania and Latvia were the cockpit for German and Polish resistance to Bolshevism. In Lithuania the capital of Vilnius was seized by the Russians and then recaptured by the Poles – a source of friction for the next 20 years. Lithuania was recognised as an independent state in 1922, but tension remained high with both Russia and Germany and in 1923 the Lithuanians seized the German port of Memel, holding onto it until it was 'liberated' by Hitler.

To the north in Estonia there was also a Russian incursion but independence was achieved in 1920. That independence was to last until the Second World War, when all three states were illegally occupied by the Soviet Union with Hitler's connivance, then invaded by the Germans and then taken back again into the Soviet Union. It was to take almost 50 years until they finally gained their freedom once more in 1990. Latvia, where Kissling served

TWO PICTURES FROM RIGA IN 1919 TAKEN BY KISSLING WHEN ON ATTACHMENT TO THE GERMAN
LEGATION DURING THE CIVIL STRIFE BEFORE INDEPENDENCE.

for two months in 1919, was destabilised by both Bolshevik troops and by the German 'Iron Guard' – a largely irregular force dedicated to fighting the spread of Bolshevism and securing traditional 'German' lands from Polish or Russian domination.

The role of the *Regierungen Estlands unde Lettlands* which Kissling joined was both military and civil and his duties reflected that dual role, as his diplomatic record in the German archives clearly shows. As a trainee his duties included shadowing the permanent staff in their liaison with German soldiers and the civilian authorities – several different administrations depending on which side of the conflict he was stationed.

When Kissling left Riga in August 1919 Latvia still had a year and a half of internal strife to endure before independence was recognised in January 1921. Almost exactly 70 years later I was fortunate enough to stand in the same square as Kissling had when he took his photographs of the centre of Riga, and again to see barricades on the streets – but this time as monuments to the defence of independence against the Russians.

From September 1919 until the summer of 1922 Kissling returned to formal study – first of all at the Freidrich-Wilhelm University in Berlin and then at the Alberts University in Königsberg. He studied international law and history, graduating with a thesis on British statecraft and foreign policy – the bound copies of which he kept in his suitcase of papers until he died.

As a 24-year-old student of independent means, with a respectable war record and a career mapped out in the Foreign Service, the young Werner Kissling led a privileged life. Even the economic horror of postwar inflation in the Weimar Republic would have left him comparatively immune from the poverty that was beginning to take root all around him. And Berlin was then an exciting, sensual place – a place where, with money and privilege, anything was possible.

Surprisingly Kissling talked little about this period of his life. There are one or two photographs in the suitcase that were probably taken during his student days but he does not seem to have been the type of person who regarded his youth as being the finest of his years. And because youth – even postponed youth as his was, with the experience of First World War service behind him – is the time of self-discovery, this later reticence may in part be explained by his discovery of his own sexuality.

In the last years of his life he had no difficulty in telling his friends that he was, and always had been, homosexual. But those whom he knew during his life – particularly those in the Western Isles – had no inkling of his sexual preference and he seems to have lived either a very discreet, or very celibate life, when in Scotland.

One can only surmise that in the early postwar days in Berlin he had discovered his own inclinations and either fulfilled them or repressed them. In the suitcase of photographs there are no letters or documents that refer to this matter, but there are one or two photographs of unnamed young men who may be relatives or friends from this period, or who may have been lovers. All we have are the sparse official records of his career, and some of his memories as told to others later in life, filtered by time and moulded by recollection and other experiences.

In the summer of 1922 he graduated and was almost immediately posted to the Consular School, which was part of the Civil Service training structure. For some of his training he was seconded to the office of the Chancellor, Gustav Stresemann. He continued to assist Stresemann when he returned to the post of Foreign Minister – his duties were later to include being part of the German delegation to the League of Nations when Germany entered that organisation in 1926.

Kissling's animosity in later life towards the Nazis was well-known and according to a number of his friends in Dumfries in the 1980s, that animosity had its roots in his experience in post-war Berlin, when the National Socialist movement was being founded. Kissling met with senior Nazis during the 'Beer Hall Putsch' of November 1922, when he was working for Stresemann. According to Kissling he had the job of meeting a Nazi delegation which came to see Stresemann during the Putsch. He waited with them in a grand reception room in the Reichstag until Stresemann was ready to receive them and he recalled their behaviour as 'boorish'. 'They were', he told one friend, 'a load of ignorant shits, who made rude jokes about the paintings and showed an incredible arrogance'.

Kissling could not have been immune to the obvious growing influence of the Nazis. He frequently referred to Hitler as 'the Boy Scout', a term of abuse that was common amongst aristocrats in Weimar Germany. It would be wrong, however, to delineate Kissling at this time as either a liberal or socialist opponent of Hitler. His background and his sympathy with Stresemann (whom he admired) indicate that he was closer to the so called 'Fulfilment' group who regarded it as necessary for Germany to meet her obligations under the Treaty of Versailles and reverse the diplomatic isolation of the country. Only by so doing could Germany become strong enough again to play a crucial role in Europe. It was Stresemann who managed to negotiate a reduction in reparations and the Allied evacuation of the Rhineland, which had been occupied after the First World War.

Stresemann's constructive approach to postwar Germany was recognised by the award of the Nobel Peace Prize in 1926, but his death in 1929 came just before his policy was overturned by the rise of Hitler. A glimpse of Kissling – 'polished, good-looking, efficient' – at the League of Nations in Geneva is given by someone who did not know him then, but who was to become one of his closest friends. Andrew Croft was visiting Geneva in 1926 and observed the League of Nations in action. He was to go on to have a highly colourful life in Arctic exploration; as the tutor to a maharajah; as a regular soldier and latterly as the commandant of the Metropolitan Police Training College in London. Croft recalls seeing Kissling in Geneva and by this time he had the official title of Vice-Consul having served in Madrid and Budapest during 1925 and the first half of 1926. His posting to Geneva lasted eight months when he was transferred to London and promoted to Second Secretary within four weeks of his arrival. A year

CARTOON OF WERNER KISSLING (LEFT). THE CARTOONIST ALSO PRESENTED HIM WITH A MENU CARTOON FROM 1917 IN GENEVA, SIGNED BY THE FUTURE CHANCELLOR OF GERMANY, GUSTAV STRESEMANN.

after his posting to London he took a few months sabbatical leave – probably to follow up his anthropological interests – but he was to remain in post in London until January 1931 when he resigned from the service and left it for ever.

Events in Germany had their influence on this decision. With Stresemann dead the restraining forces on extremism in Germany were weakening. As early as 1926 Goebbels had become gauleiter of Berlin and as head of the party in Germany's capital city, it became a haven for political bully boys. In 1930 the Nazis won 107 seats in the Reichstag and the German financial crisis deepened with every passing day. The following year all the banks closed and economic conditions for ordinary Germans were either dire or ludicrous. At the same time Kissling was pursuing his amateur interests in photography and ethnology with greater and greater vigour: he had certainly paid a first visit to the Western Isles and to the West Coast of Scotland sometime in 1928 and returned again the following year. He had met and was involved with a circle of ethnologists based in Cambridge and had started research on the Hebridean black house, a project that was to fascinate him for many years.

Ethnology was a fashionable occupation in the 1930s, and was a good antidote to the race-based ethnic studies that so obsessed the Nazis. Both interests had a common root – the desire to examine the origins of present-day society. But for those who abhorred prejudice and ignorance and wanted real answers, the study of people and their ways of living was a more attractive proposition than attempting to prove the superiority of one race over another.

Both Andrew Croft and some of Kissling's friends in Dumfries, including his executor David Lockwood, were told by Kissling of the circumstances surrounding his departure from the German diplomatic service. According to these stories Kissling had taken a phone call from Adolf Hitler when he became Chancellor in 1933. Hitler summoned Kissling home, claiming that his 'regiment needed him' and that failure to return would mean that he was a 'traitor to Germany'. Kissling maintained that he told Hitler that he would never be a traitor to Germany, but that Hitler was not Germany and could not speak for it. Shortly afterwards he was called in to see the German ambassador and placed under arrest. However, he claims to have evaded the two officers who were accompanying him as he left the embassy by throwing his coat over one of them and running to a waiting car, driven by Cambridge friends, which was waiting to take him away. It is a wonderful and dramatic story, and indeed Andrew Croft uses it prominently in his autobiography *A Talent For Adventure*. Unfortunately it does not seem to be true, at least in the version that Kissling told.

For a start the official records show him leaving the service on January 14, 1931 – two years before Hitler became Chancellor. The German phrase in

WERNER KISSLING AT BARMOUTH, NORTH WALES IN 1929 WHEN HE WAS SERVING AT THE GERMAN EMBASSY

Kissling's record for this departure is *…auf eigenen Antrag aus dem Reichsdienst entlassen…*[1] which clearly states resignation, or at least acceptance of the end of his service. And there is no corroboration of Kissling's story available anywhere apart from in his own account.

But perhaps the truth lies somewhere between the facts and the dramatic story. As someone known to the Nazis, and with distinguished and wealthy antecedents, he would have been a considerable catch for the Nazi party. It is not outwith the bounds of possibility that he was subject to a recruitment attempt that may have included a personal approach from Hitler who had by this time charmed many distinguished Germans, not least the business community. His rejection of the attempt would certainly have made him a marked man and someone may have persuaded him to get out whilst the chance existed. As a man of independent means, leaving paid employment would have not have worried him unduly and the prospect of developing his studies and his photography would have been all the more attractive to him.

Whatever the truth is, by the early 1930s Kissling was no longer working as a diplomat but was something of a freelance academic, able to finance his studies and travels from his own resources. Meanwhile, at home, his elder brother was running the family businesses and in the words of his nephew, 'making the money, whilst Werner and his mother spent it'. Tensions within the family over these matters were so great that Georg Conrad, his wife and three children moved from the family house at Heizendorf to a smaller (though still grand) country house at Bolkohof about 20 kilometres away, sometime after the birth of their daughter Dagmar in August 1924.

Now Werner was about to start spending even more, and was setting in motion the events that would lead to his unwitting place in Scottish film history.

---

[1] . . . resigned from the Reich service at his own request . . .

WERNER KISSLING ON BOARD THE *ELSPETH*, ERISKAY, 1934.

CHAPTER 7

Eriskay, 1934

Accepting that Werner Kissling left the German diplomatic service on January 14, 1931 rather than sometime after January 30, 1933 gives anyone writing about Kissling's life something of a problem. He certainly spent time at Cambridge where he quickly found a flat and became associated with the Department of Ethnology. But even there the documentation is sparse – his sole project appears to have been the work he was doing on the Hebridean black house and his two articles on the subject were finally published in 1944 and 1946.

Andrew Croft – whom I last mentioned as a student visiting the League of Nations – had his first proper meeting with Kissling at Cambridge, but this was not until 1936, two years after he had made the Eriskay film. Kissling probably spent time with his mother at Heizendorf, accepting that the threat to him regarding arrest if he returned to Germany was still not overwhelming. That was only likely to have been the case after January 1933 and in particular after 1935 when the draft was re-introduced and he could have been called back to military service, even at the age of 40.

Whatever the detail of his day-to-day activities, it is certain at this time that Kissling was getting to know more about the Western Isles and the life of the people who lived there. His particular interest in the small island of Eriskay, situated just off the southern tip of South Uist within sight of Barra was also beginning at this time.

Eriskay was in some senses an obvious choice for Kissling's attention. The Eriskay Love Lilt – Marjory Kennedy Fraser's most famous re-working of 'traditional melody with appropriate harmonic setting' which was part of her collection *Songs of the Hebrides*, published in 1909 – was widely known. In addition the folklore work of Fr Allan MacDonald, the parish priest of Eriskay between 1894 and 1905, had been widely reported (and perverted from time to time, most notably by Ada Goodrich-Freer). Fr MacDonald was also the correspondent and source of information for a whole range of those whom Kissling would have known of in the ethnology field, including Alexander Carmichael who contributed a chapter on land customs to Skene's

Celtic Scotland, a book that Kissling certainly had read. He was also the original for Fr Ludovic in Neil Munro's *Children of the Tempest*.

Eriskay in the thirties was also the site of much research on Gaelic storytelling and song (the Irish Folklore Commission, for example, collected on Eriskay as well as elsewhere in the Western Isles) and the people of Eriskay were used to being visited in their role of Gaelic archetypes. The traditional nature of Gaelic society on Eriskay and its continuing use of methods of the past would have also attracted Kissling in his search for actual examples of black houses still in use – a comparatively rare phenomenon even in the 1930s because of the rash of house improvements introduced from the 1890s onwards.

It is likely that Kissling first visited Eriskay before he made his film in 1934, if only to check out the lie of the land and make sure that those things he was interested in still existed on the island. But his intentions on Eriskay probably remained in the area of photography and written recording as adjuncts of his studies until the spring of 1934, when he came in contact with the phenomenon of Robert Flaherty and his film *Man of Aran*.

Flaherty was one of the most colourful film makers of his generation. Born in Iron Mountain, Michigan in 1884 he was originally an explorer until, almost accidentally, he made his first film *Nanook of the North* when his sponsor for an expedition suggested he took a 'new fangled invention – the motion picture camera'. Released finally in 1922 after many years development, Nanook was a sensational success. Paul Rotha has said that 'documentary may be said to have had its real beginning's with Flaherty's Nanook', but by the early 1930s Flaherty had shifted his focus from the Arctic and the Pacific, where he had co-directed White Shadows on the South Seas, to the British Isles. After co-directing Industrial Britain he was commissioned by Michael Balcon of British Gaumont Pictures to make a mammoth epic on the Aran Islands in Galway Bay, a film that was to be released in 1934 as *Man of Aran*.

Even with the pressure of modern tourism, and the powerful boats that arrive every hour from Rossaveil, it is not difficult to be captured by the uniqueness of the Aran Islands. Strip away the jaunting carts and the flocks of hired bicycles, narrow your eyes to eliminate the new bungalows on the horizon and the islands are still the most curious landscape, a patchwork of tiny fields hewn from the rock with soil built layer upon layer by the application of seaweed.

Aran and Eriskay both drew writers, artists and those interested in traditional Gaelic life. For Aran the originator of the movement to observe and record was J M Synge, and although Flaherty's film is the best known artefact from that movement, there have been – and continue to be – many others. Flaherty's commitment to primitivism was on celluloid, rather than in real life. He imported onto the island a cordon bleu chef and during his stay one islander observed that 'there is more thrown out of his house, they say, then would give food to half the villages in the island. Where there are quarters of beef and quarters of mutton and millions of tins of everything that come from every land on which the sun shines'.

Flaherty's spent two years living on Inis Mor, the largest of the Aran Islands and by the end of that time he was simply repeating himself, still worrying away at shots which were already complete and waiting for editing. Shooting only finished when Michael Balcon forcibly recalled him to London, where Gaumont Pictures was beginning to despair of ever seeing a finished product. The film had been intended to be silent, but technology had moved on since it was first conceived and three of the main protagonists were taken to London to add snatches of dialogue to a soundtrack. It was a technique which Kissling himself was to use for his film.

The première of *Man of Aran* took place on April 25, 1934 at the New Gallery in London. It was certainly the event of the season, with the audience in evening dress, islanders in their native homespun, the band of the Irish Guards and even a stuffed basking shark displayed in the window of the Gaumont Pictures London offices. The latter displeased Flaherty because the middle of the shark had to be cut out to accommodate the rest of the display, somewhat diminishing the impact of the beast!

Although we have no documented evidence to prove Kissling's presence at this event, some years afterwards he confided in a friend that it had been *Man of Aran* that had inspired him to take a professional movie camera to Eriskay for his 1934 trip. He had in mind, apparently, a first sketch or essay in film making which would be useful in preparing a much longer and more complete documentary on traditional life in the Western Isles – a sort of 'Man of Eriskay', but with a closer attention to scholarly detail. This film would form part of his studies of the Hebrides, illuminating more than a mere article.

Kissling was, first and foremost, a scholar. His subsequent work in the Dumfries Museum, the articles he wrote and the meticulous presentation of the minutiae of traditional crafts have the hallmark of academic scrutiny. So does, as we have seen, his original script for *A Poem Of Remote Lives*.

It is this scholarly approach that perhaps makes his only film more of a record – an invaluable one, certainly, and an entertaining one - than a documentary that breaks barriers: narrative line is sketchy in the film as we have it and the technique is often that of a stills photographer. So it might be fair to place him at one end of the spectrum of documentary production (the 'recorder') and seek places in other parts of that spectrum for Flaherty and for another documentary film maker active in the year that Kissling put hand to camera – Leni Riefensthal.

Although Riefensthal's most celebrated work *Triumph of the Will* was only in production when Kissling was working on Eriskay, it is likely he knew of her, and of her project. Originally an actress, she had made her first film in 1931 and was acclaimed for an original eye and a genius in editing. Tainted for virtually all her life because of her associations with the Nazis – she was shunned by the film-making community after the Second World War, but only died in 1993 – her film of the 1934 Nuremberg Rally was commissioned by Hitler, and remains the most stylish and stylistic documentary essay of its period.

But style is not all. Riefensthal in her film became a propagandist, not a recorder. The film was intended to breathe monumental significance into the Nazi play acting, and to relate it to a movement that would change a people and the world. It was a film made from a standpoint, for a purpose – a film in which the manipulation of images was used to build a wave of emotion to support a point of view. As one critic has said, 'After *Triumph of the Will* film makers could no longer be passive observers . . . their medium would inherit a whole new scrutiny.' So whereas Kissling was a 'recorder and observer', Riefensthal was a 'manipulator'. And Flaherty stood somewhere between the two.

For Flaherty invented much of his subjects' lives – not because he needed fiction, but because fact needed to be treated selectively and creatively in order to make a true story of power and inspiration. In defence of Flaherty's technique Dudley Andrews argued that 'all the fabrications were calculated attempts to make the images on the screen breathe the truth of a way of life that goes beyond immediate experiences. Flaherty believed that appearances must often be transformed from life to the screen (indeed events must be altered) if the equation of a man's life in his environment is to retain its essential significance'.

Graham Greene was scathing of *Man of Aran* saying in one review that it 'did not even attempt to describe truthfully a way of life'. John Grierson – a Scot and a friend of Flaherty's – was somewhat critical too, writing that: 'I like my braveries to emerge otherwise than from the sea, and stand otherwise than against the sky. I imagine they shine as bravely in the pursuit of Irish landlords as in the pursuit of Irish sharks'. Flaherty was a undoubtedly a 'dramatist' within the recording of documentary tradition, but he was also manipulative. He lies in the middle of this spectrum of the tradition, and Kissling, as he prepares to sail to his island, is inspired by that dramatic treatment, and that attempt to find 'essential significance' in the lives of his subjects.

There may have been at least one further influence on Kissling's growing determination to make a film on Eriskay. In an era of mass communication, where any number of documentaries are daily available on a multiplicity of channels, it is sometimes difficult to imagine a time when the documentary was an emerging genre. But the 1930s was that time, and its emergence owes a great deal to the inspired creation of the GPO Film Unit which, by 1934, was established in Soho Square, London, under the supervision of John Grierson.

Grierson attracted around him a wealth of talent. Film makers like Alberto Cavalcanti, writers like WH Auden, musicians like Brittan and Milhaud, cameramen of the like of Frank 'Jonah' Jones all worked together, sometimes taking on different roles (Cavalcanti edited, directed and produced, for example) and producing documentaries that established the art form as we know it. *Night Mail*, made in 1936, is probably the best known of those early productions but there were many others and the unit reflected the fascination with the sea and 'remoteness' that had inspired Flaherty too. Indeed Flaherty himself worked with the unit, encouraging younger talent for a while.

Eriskay itself was included in the unit's film *Islanders*, made by Maurice Harvey, which compared communication in Eriskay, Guernsey and the Farne Islands, although the portrayal of the island is much more conventional, and has much less insight than Kissling's portrait. However it does use some Gaelic actuality – probably only the second time that some of the islanders had found themselves recorded and had had the opportunity of seeing themselves and their lives on the screen.

And given the theatrical distribution of these films (and the non-theatrical distribution to countless societies and social evenings) Kissling must have been familiar with the work of the unit, and the way in which Grierson and his colleagues represented reality would have been deeply attractive to him and probably very influential.

Having decided to use film as well as photography on his visit to Eriskay in 1934, Kissling purchased the necessary equipment: an easy task for a man of substance, though the cost would have been significant, nonetheless. He certainly bought a 35mm camera – the largest professional format available to him. As previously stated he also had some form of sound recording equipment, for both the actuality he witnessed and for some of the background Gaelic conversation. The film shows no interiors, and because powerful lights would have required electricity which was not available on

THE CAPTAIN OF THE *ELSPETH,* THE 'SKYEMAN'. NOTE THE MISSING FINGER ON HIS RIGHT HAND.

THE 'CREW' OF THE *ELSPETH.* ONE OF THE TWO FIGURES NEAREST THE CAMERA MAY WELL HAVE BEEN 'THE VALET'.

the island in 1934, portable lighting was clearly out of the question. Kissling's interior photographs from Eriskay, taken at the same time, show an acute sensitivity to the power of light and shade, but the technology of the time did not allow him to replicate that on film.

Sometime in the early summer of 1934 Werner Kissling travelled north to Glasgow, where he chartered the Gourock-registered sailing yacht, the *Elspeth*. With the yacht came a skipper, and with Kissling came a valet – or at least that is how the people of Eriskay remember Kissling's companion. They also remember at least two other men on the yacht, though whether these were crew or friends of Kissling, and whether they were a permanent fixture during the summer on the island is not known.

The precise date of Kissling's visit to Eriskay is similarly vague. The film depicts transporting peats, sheep, shearing and crop harvesting and so it would appear that the visit may have started in late June or early July, depending on the weather that summer, and continued until at least the beginning of September.

We must assume that Kissling sailed from Greenock, a journey which – as an experienced seaman – he would have found stimulating or terrifying, depending on the weather. There is no film of the journey, at least not in the final edit, which suggests that it was either too rough, or not interesting enough, although the voyage would have taken them – on the most direct routing – through the Crinan Canal, and between many of the islands that make up the Inner Hebrides (see photograph below). Perhaps the lack of this aspect in the film indicates how focused Kissling was on the project. It was not to turn into, or edge towards, the 'travelogue', at least not until his editor got his hands on it, and persuaded Kissling to add the flowery introduction.

Anchorages on Eriskay for a yacht of the size of Kissling's have to be selected with care. Hamish Haswell-Smith's excellent and comprehensive 1996 guide to Scotland's islands identifies only two choices – Acairseid Mhor, the main harbour, and Haun, where the present car ferry docks from Uist. Haun is 'not recommended' because of its 'very shallow and difficult approach through rocks and sandbanks'. The film, as we have discussed earlier, includes footage of the yacht entering into the small harbour at Eriskay at Acairseid Mhor (including navigation instructions being called by one of the people on the yacht, no doubt to avoid the 'drying rocks at entrance' referred to by Haswell-Smith) and accordingly that anchorage must have been used. Some people on the island also remember the yacht moored off the Prince's Bay, and it is likely that it was used by Kissling and his party during their stay to travel further afield to South Uist, Barra and perhaps down to Mingulay.

However we also know that Kissling took lodgings on the island, staying in Ronald MacInnes' house, one of the best in the island, and sleeping in one of the small upstairs rooms. The house would have had no electricity or running water , but it had a toilet down by the shore – a small shed, doubtless with a practical and essential supply of the *Sunday Post* or some such newspaper. There are still people alive on Eriskay who remember Kissling and his visit in 1934. He had a 'wind-up gramophone' on which he used to play classical music (presumably including Mahler's 3rd Symphony which was his favourite), and children in particular were invited to visit the yacht – although according to Peggy MacMillan: 'He took us out to go aboard, but there was someone who did not want us to get on board, and we never got onto it – so that was that!'

During his visit he spent a great deal of time visiting – going round

TOBERMORY, MULL, EN ROUTE TO ERISKAY. THE BUSTLING
PORT APPEARS MUCH AS IT IS TODAY.

RONALD MACINNES' HOUSE WHERE KISSLING
STAYED DURING HIS VISIT.

the houses. But as he also paid further visits after 1934 (and probably at least one before then) some of the memories are conflated. For example, he stayed on the island with a Mrs Johnstone on several occasions after his filming visit, and again was active in visiting and talking with local people. As we shall see, it was the problems and difficulties of island life that he discovered in those visits that motivated him to later become a type of 'advocate' for the island community.

His visits to local people were usually connected with traditional crafts. He filmed and photographed a number of islanders at work, including Bean Iagain Mhoir who was an expert in spinning and waulking.[1] And although the famous 'Eriskay jersey' does not feature in the film, he took a keen interest in the production of these items, making suggestions about their marketing that were not to come to fruition until the late 1970s. Then, a co-operative was formed that took control of this valuable product and started to return to the islanders more than the fraction of the sale price that they previously obtained.

I still have in my wardrobe one of the Eriskay jerseys, sold to me for £20 by one of the knitters at a time when they were fetching three times that amount in New York department stores. Somewhat too small for me now, it is still a wonderful example of the intricate use of traditional patterns such as the tree of life and the anchor. Each of the patterns used has a meaning for the knitters and each jersey blends them uniquely, giving a signature of the woman who made it.

The jerseys are superbly practical garments – warm for fishing and ideal for those exposed to the ever-changing island weather – as well as individual works of art. The fact that they are so little known in Scotland today shows how much we have become influenced from south of our borders, and how little by what lies within them to the north and west.

Kissling is reputed to have kept a daily diary when on Eriskay in 1934, but it does not exist in any of the archives that hold his papers, and it was not in the suitcase which he left behind, so it is not possible to do any more than attempt a reconstruction of his filming visit, using the film itself as evidence.

The bulk of the population of Eriskay live in the north of the island, scattered around Haun and the ferry link to South Uist. Most of the filming takes place in this area, and along the road (then a track) that leads south to Acairseid Mhor. Surprisingly, given the focus of the latter half of the film on wool and its preparation for weaving, there are no shots of weaving itself. It may be that the interiors where the looms were located were too dark to allow filming but Kissling certainly was interested in the process and as part of his advocacy in later years, wished to see it invested in.

Even with the difficulty of telling exactly what the weather was for filming (the grainy black and white print does not give many clues) it does seems as if Kissling was reliant totally on natural light and accordingly was unable to film in conditions which had given Flaherty's film such violent authenticity.

This is a pity since the idyllic nature of many of the shots belies the actuality of Eriskay and the Western Isles even in the best of summers. There is a long shot of a hillside in what appears to be typical summer fog, with the cloud level below the tops of the hills, but there are no shots that suggest gales or high winds, which are typical of the Western Isles in all but the best of weathers. Even if the summer of 1934 was warm and tranquil, there would still have been days of rain and days when outdoor work was uncomfortable, if not impossible. Certainly in the autumn (particularly around the end of September when the equinoctial gales can blow for days on end) the weather would have deteriorated and because all the filming and activities that are observed are those of summer, we have to conclude that Kissling's trip finished at the latest in mid-September and that the *Elspeth* would have been safely back in the Clyde before the autumn winds started to blow.

Kissling must therefore have spent at most just over two months, and at least six weeks on Eriskay during the summer of 1934. Now he had the task of editing his film and allowing a skilled midwife to mine out the best of what he had shot. And although he could not have known it at the time, Kissling had now completed what was to be the most memorable part of his life's work.

[1] Seen in the portrait on page 84 and in the images on pages 82 and 94.

UNIVERSITY MUSEUM
OF ARCHÆOLOGY AND ETHNOLOGY,
CAMBRIDGE.

14th. December, 1938

Dr. W. Kissling, who is a research student in
the University of Cambridge, and is also in charge of
the Lantern slide collection in the University Museum
of Archaeology and Ethnology, is on his way to New
Zealand where he is to do some ethnological research work
for the Museum. This work will include the taking of
Photographic records for the Museum Collection.

Any help given to Dr. Kissling will be appreciated
by

A. C. Haddon

Emeritus Reader in Ethnology in the
University of Cambridge

A LETTER OF INTRODUCTION CONFIRMING KISSLING'S POSITION AT
CAMBRIDGE UNIVERSITY PRIOR TO HIS VISIT TO NEW ZEALAND.

CHAPTER 8

Scholar and Gentleman

Soldier, Diplomat, Scholar and Gentleman states Kissling's gravestone in St Michael's Kirkyard in Dumfries. The words were chosen by Ralph Coleman, an amateur antiquarian in Dumfries and a friend and confidante of Kissling. Those four, short, words aptly describe aspects of Werner Kissling's life and character which neatly categorise many of his achievements. But the addition of the words 'Photographer and Film Maker' are much needed, for it is in those areas that Kissling shone more brightly than many of his contemporaries in the other callings.

But he had a scholarly, gentlemanly approach even to film and photography. Kissling's essentially academic approach to his lifetime interest in people and places is evidenced, as we have seen, by his single film, by his role as an 'observer' and by his many photographs of Eriskay and South Uist. Even after the première of *A Poem Of Remote Lives* Kissling continued to see photography as an adjunct to his academic pursuits, rather than a creative activity in itself.

He was elected as a Fellow of the Royal Anthropological Institute of Great Britain and Ireland on April 28, 1931 and his letter of admission, dated the following day, was one of his most prized possessions. He also kept his letter of admission as a Fellow of the Royal Geographical Society, en event that had taken place in June the preceding year.

These steps into his chosen field indicate that during his time in the German embassy in London he was already becoming known for his other interests. Coming so close to his 'retiral' from the diplomatic service, it suggests even more strongly that the events were connected: Kissling's private wealth allowed him to pursue his chosen studies free of the obligations and distractions of daily work.

From 1931 onwards he seems to have lived most of the time in Cambridge, taking a small flat (which he kept until he moved to Melrose) and in London where he had a house in Manor Street, Chelsea. During the 1930s he was enrolled as a research student in Cambridge, working primarily on a study of the Hebridean black house while developing a keen interest in photography.

The life of a wealthy postgraduate student would have been a pleasant one, particularly with Kissling's social contacts. And if he had wished it, there was the chance of continuing contact with the intellectual life of Germany before the rise of Fascism. At Cambridge itself Wittgenstein was teaching and writing, and the many similarities between them (homosexual, academic, reserved but interested in what went on around them) makes it possible that they knew each other. There were other 'émigrés' too, although Kissling so fully absorbed life in England it is doubtful that he ultimately saw himself as anything other than a type of English gentleman. Certainly he could afford to be one, and his studies and surroundings enhanced the role of 'gentleman scholar' that he had found for himself.

Indeed his whole focus seems to have been on his academic life. In a letter date August 1, 1942 to Andrew Croft (whom he had met in 1936 in Cambridge) he refers to the film as having been 'made for the Cambridge Museum in 1936 and subsequently released for General Exhibition', which

ANDREW AND ROSALIND CROFT AT THEIR THAMES-SIDE HOME,
IN THE LATE 1970s.

does not accord with the actual production and distribution dates, still less with the billing of the film for its premiere, although it does confirm that the purpose of the film was connected closely with his studies.

He also confirms that 'my researches in ethnology and sociology have centred largely in the Outer Hebrides, and have entailed numerous extended visits since 1934. By living as a member of the community, I have obtained a first-hand understanding of conditions in South Uist and Eriskay, some of the results of which are being incorporated in a Cambridge Thesis'.

Theses aside, a letter dated December 14, 1938 and signed by the 'Emeritus Reader in Ethnology in the University of Cambridge' describes him as 'in charge of the Lantern Slide collection in the University Museum of Archaeology and Ethnology' and his experience of photography must have recommended him for that task.

Whilst we can very precisely place his whereabouts and activities from the period June 1934 through to the spring of 1935 – he was working on his film either in Eriskay or in Bush House in London – it is difficult to be precise about other periods of time during the 1930s. His 'extended visits' to the islands certainly took place and there is some local memory of him bringing his photographs to Eriskay in 1935, along with the film, and it would have been typical of him to arrange a local showing. He returned again the following year and busied himself with enquiries both into the history and architecture of the black house and also with the details of modern life on the island. He wanted the government to invest in weaving, and was also concerned that the island had no running water. In particular the school was deprived of that and other facilities, the lack of which he regarded as dangerous to health.

In 1937 he started to write letters about these problems – letters to the Scottish Office, to MPs and ministers, to the headquarters of the local authority in distant Inverness – and to the newspapers. He kept in close contact with community leaders in South Uist and Eriskay, writing to the priests and school teachers and receiving letters, information and unsolicited complaints from local families. He began working as the self-appointed mouthpiece of the community in an attempt to have modern facilities provided. An example of his concerns can be found in a letter published in the *Daily Telegraph* and the *Morning Post* on December 4, 1937:

Remembering your kindness to the people of Eriskay, which the islanders deeply appreciated, I though that you would like to know the present position.

On my recent annual visit to the Outer Hebrides I visited Eriskay again. The islanders seem in a more hopeful mood, since a small sum of money provided by a film record of their life which I succeeded in making had been utilised for constructing a road on the island, so that the use of a horse and cart for the supply of fresh water had relieved those who used to carry their water by hand from house to house.

Now this community of 470 is hoping to obtain a water supply for their school and townships. The present conditions are far from hygienic. Houses and byres are clustered round the wells, so that there is a permanent danger of contamination. The wells frequently dry up in summer and the islanders have to go one mile up a hill to fetch a bucket of water from a loch.

In the school a small tank of rain water, with all its impurities, has to supply a hundred children. Even if the water were healthy, it is insufficient. With a diet mainly of salt fish and potatoes , the demand for drinking water is considerable , and fear of typhoid through infection from water cannot easily be dismissed. An adequate water supply for the island would not involve public expense of more than two or three thousand pounds.

May I give expression to my hope that this small community of great mental power and courage will manage to remain on their native island, and that encouragement of their home industry, the hand spinning of tweeds, will support them in their hard struggle for existence?

Yours faithfully, WERNER KISSLING.

Most of the information in the letter comes from work done by a local school teacher, who sent him not only the details of the positioning of the wells, but also an analysis of where they were and what ground conditions prevailed.

He wrote also to people whom he knew, or knew of. Malcolm MacDonald, Ramsay MacDonald's son was Dominion Secretary at the time, and Kissling addresses him as 'Dear MacDonald', and goes on to claim that he had talked to his 'father on more than one occasion when I saw him at Lossiemouth, and to our mutual friend Mrs Graham-Murray' regarding another of his concerns: the need for investment in the island fishing fleet.

But from his base in Cambridge, even with a network of influential friends, his campaign began to look more and more like patronising eccentricity. He tells Malcolm MacDonald that the 'Secretary of State for Scotland (Sir Walter Elliot) is looking into the matter of the water supply for the school' and then adds:

If you would like to see me in this matter at any time, please tell me at 60 Manor St, SW3, Tel Flaxman 0725 as I visit the Island so often that I might be able to explain things to you.

However the letter got a reply only via the local MP, Malcolm K MacMillan, to whom the Dominion Secretary had sent it. Malcolm K's response makes it clear that he is agitating on behalf of the islanders as well, though he does confirm that he 'very much appreciates your very sincere and lasting interest in the welfare of the people of Eriskay' and then confirms that he himself has been unable to get there so far, but hopes to be there in April.

Kissling even enlisted the help of his friends in the crusade, sending them copy letters from fishermen, and anonymous 'elder sons' of families. Good and faithful friend that he is, Andrew Croft takes up the cudgels and is still at it in 1942 when the Scottish Office is forced to remind him of the 'serious shortage of labour and materials' that would have to be taken into account when considering whether anything could be done at 'the present time'.

What improvements there were came slowly and largely – though not entirely – without his prompting. The supply of piped water to the whole of the Western Isles was a project already in its infancy, and would be completed, after the interruption of war, in the 1950s. Electricity came later, but more rapidly, as a by-product of Tom Johnstone's drive for the electrification and improvement of rural Scotland. Better housing was already underway, and the black house was all but extinct as a domestic dwelling by the start of the Second World War, although a few continued to be inhabited in parts of the Western Isles until the 1970s.

During the late 1930s Kissling developed an interest in the Maori culture of New Zealand and left Cambridge on a study visit at the end of 1938. Some of the photographs he took in New Zealand still exist in the Museum of Mankind in London and in some other collections, but whilst they are dramatic and striking, they seem tied almost too closely to the ethnological aims of his visit, and have little of the vitality and character of the Western Isles pictures. Arriving back in England in September 1939, Kissling was immediately arrested and interned in the Tower of London – his status as former German diplomat ensured that he would be under considerable suspicion. But his network of friends in high places was still extant: within 24 hours Andrew Croft had demanded to see Lord Birkenhead and in fury told him that Werner's record in opposition to Hitler and the Nazi's made his arrest intolerable and unjust. He was released, but not without conditions: he was sent to the large scale internment camp on the Isle of Man where he worked as a welfare officer, still under restriction.

The camp contained many individuals who had made their lives in Britain, and for whom internment appeared unjust and a form of victimisation. Amongst those in the camp was Charles Forte who founded the famous hotel chain. Others included relatives of Count Ciano, the Italian Foreign Minister, whose only crime whilst running their catering business in North Wales was to have been so unlucky in their relations.

After almost three years, Kissling was released and returned to his flat in Causewayside, Cambridge. However he was not permitted to return to the Western Isles during the war years. Despite testimonials from the local priests and from other individuals who knew him, the Western Isles remained a security zone from which foreign nationals and those without good reason to be there, were excluded. Financially he appears still to have been self-sufficient, but the events of the war were touching him directly. His elder brother Georg Conrad had remained in Germany and entered the army again at the start of the war. Promoted to the rank of major, he was working in a staff position on July 20, 1944, the day of the ill-fated July Plot.

The plot was designed to eliminate Hitler and place in power a more moderate government which could negotiate peace. However, owing to a combination of bad luck and some disorganisation (Hitler was only wounded, not killed and the telephone lines to Hitler's headquarters at Rastenburg were not cut according to the plan) the conspiracy failed. Energetic action by the SS Major Ernest Remer in Berlin foiled the takeover of power, and a wave of arrests followed. Some 15 of those involved committed suicide, including Georg Conrad Kissling who was arrested the day after the bomb explosion. His adjutant handed him his service revolver and Georg immediately took his own life.

The effect on the Kissling family in Germany was immediate. Werner kept in the suitcase some letters from that time including a note of his brother's burial, an expulsion order from the Gestapo ordering his family to leave their home and a letter from the family solicitor, outlining the legal problems that existed for them. Whilst Bolkohof, the smaller of the family houses, had remained as a private house, Heizendorf had long since been taken over for military use for the duration of the war: now neither residence was available and indeed would never be again.

Johanna Kissling was now living in Wiesbaden, a prosperous spa city on the Rhine near Frankfurt. But Wiesbaden was being regularly bombed by the Allies and was badly damaged. Frau Kissling was not safe there and Werner was becoming increasingly worried about her, and about her future. Sometime in 1945 he concocted a plan with Andrew Croft to get his mother out of Germany to join him in Cambridge. The plan was not possible to execute during the war, but immediately afterwards Croft's brother-in-law (another Polar explorer) succeeded in meeting Frau Kissling in Austria and smuggled her back to London under the nose of the occupying authorities.

Frau Kissling settled into her son's flat in Cambridge, but was not keen on joining him on his travels. After 1946 he was again allowed to visit the Western Isles, and his trips began to have the routine about them which he liked. He would motor in his little black Austin from Cambridge to Oban or Mallaig, taking his time and stopping to visit some of the vast circle of friends he had accumulated from London society and academic life. He had a way of engaging people and striking up acquaintanceships which is largely lost in modern society. Friends whom he might see a dozen times or less in his life, but with whom he would exchange the odd letter were attracted to the aristocratic independence of his manner, allied to an easy informality and his quick and enquiring intelligence.

During the late 1940s and early 1950s he spent time in Argyll, Edinburgh and the Borders, staying with friends or lodging in hotels. Once

Abschrift

Oberkommando der Wehrmacht   Berlin W 35, den 3. 8. 44
Wehrersatzamt / Abt. E   Tirpitzufer 72-76

                        Frau
                        A. Kissling
                        Bolkohof   über Trebnitz
                              (Schlesien)

            Hiermit erfüllt die Dienststelle die
traurige Pflicht, Ihnen von dem am 22.7. durch
Freitod erfolgten Ableben Ihres Herrn Gemahl Kennt-
nis zu geben.

            Die Beisetzung hat in aller Stille am
27.7. auf dem Alten Garnison-Friedhof, Berlin SW 29,
Columbiastrasse, Hasenheide stattgefunden. Die Grab-
stätte befindet sich im Feld 32, Reihe 1, Grabstelle 1.

                        Heil Hitler!
                            J.A.

                        gez. Herbert
                        Hauptmann u. Bürooffizier

Anlage
4 Todesbescheinigungen

Abschrift.

Geheime Staatspolizei   Breslau, den 2.September 1944
Staatspolizeistelle Breslau   Anger 10
Br. Nr. IV 1 b - 31880/44 g.

An die Firma
Konrad Kißling
in Breslau
Junkernstr. 15 .   Geheim!

     Auf Grund des § 1 der Verordnung des Herrn Reichspräsidenten zum
Schutze von Volk und Staat vom 28.2.33 (RGBl. I S. 83) in Verbindung mit
§ 1 des Gesetzes über die Geheime Staatspolizei von 10.2.1936 (Preuss.
Gesetzsammlung Seite 21) wird mit sofortiger Wirkung das gesamte
Vermögen der nachstehend Genannten staatspolizeilich sichergestellt:
1. Major Georg Konrad Kissling, geb. 20.7.93 in Breslau, zuletzt wohnhaft
   Bolkohof über Trebnitz (verstorben)
2. Frau Alice Kissling geb. von Printz, geb. 11.11.96, z.Zt. in Schutzhaft
   als Ehegattin,
3. Georg Konrad Kissling, geb. 28.2,4,20 , Leutnant d.R. z.Zt. vermisst,
4. Peter Joachim Kissling, geb. 1.6.21, Oberleutnant, z.Zt. im Felde,
5. Dagmar Kissling, geb. 14.8.24, zur Zt. Landfrauenschule Peterhof über
   Zobten.
     Die Verwaltung der sichergestellten Vermögenswerte liegt ab sofort in
Händen des Herrn Oberfinanzpräsidenten Niederschlesien, Breslau 18,
Hardenbergstr. 9/11, der nunmehr allein verfügungsberechtigt ist.
     Bei einer Zuwiderhandlung gegen diese Verfügung erfolgt Bestrafung
gemäss § 4 der Verordnung des Reichspräsidenten vom 28. .33.
Die Höhe des Geschäftsanteils des verstorbenen Majors Georg Konrad Kiss-
ling ist umgehend mitzuteilen.
                              gez. Dr. Scharpwinkel
                              SS-Obersturmbannführer

                        LS   Beglaubigt
                              gez. Unterschrift
                              Kriminalinspektor

THE LETTER INTIMATING TO GEORG CONRAD'S WIFE ALICE OF HIS
SUICIDE IN THE WAKE OF THE JULY PLOT.

THE TRANSLATION IS OPPOSITE

THE GESTAPO EDICT WHICH EFFECTIVELY CLAIMED THE KISSLING'S
ESTATE FOR THE NAZIS.

THE TRANSLATION IS FAR RIGHT

<u>C o p y</u>

Headquarters of the Wehrmacht   Berlin W 35, 3.8.44
<u>Military Recruitment Agency / Dept. E</u>   Tirpitzufer 72-76

Mrs A. K i s s l i n g
<u>B o l k o h o f by Trebnitz</u>
(Silesia)

The above office herewith fulfills its sad duty to inform you that your husband has taken his own life on 22.7.

It was a quiet funeral which took place at the Alten Garnison-Friedhof, Berlin SW 29 Columbiastrasse, Hasenheide, on 27.7. The grave is located in field 32, row 1, grave 1.

Heil Hitler!

on behalf
pp. H e r b e r t
Captain and Senior Office Clerk

<u>Enclosure</u>
4 death certificates

<u>Copy</u>

Gestapo   Breslau 2nd September 1944
Police Department Breslau   Anger 10

<u>Br. No. IV 1 b - 31480/44 g</u>

                                                 Signature

Messrs. Konrad Kißling

<u>Breslau</u>
Junkernstr. 15   Confidential!

        in accordance with para 1 of the Reichspräsident´s decree for the protection of the people and the state of 28.2.33 (RGBL. I. Page 83) in conjunction with para 1 of the Law on the Gestapo of 10.2.1936 (Prussian compilation of laws, page 31) the entire estate of the below mentioned persons has been secured by the Gestapo with immediate effect:

1. Major Georg Konrad Kissling, born 20.7.93 in Breslau, last residence Bolkohof by Trebnitz (deceased)
2. Frau Alice Kissling, née von Printz, born 11.11.96, at present in preventive detention as wife
3. Georg Konrad Kissling, born 2.4.20 Lieutenant (reserve), at present missing
4. Peter Joachim Kissling, born 1.6.21 First Lieutenant, at present at battle
5. Dagmar Kissling, born 14.8.24, at present Agricultural College for Women Peterhof by Zobten
        With immediate effect the President of the Regional Finance Office of Lower Silesia, Breslau 18, Hardenbergstr. 9/11 is in charge of the administration of the secured estate and has sole authorisation to dispose of same.
        In the event of a violation of this disposition a penalty will be inflicted in accordance with para 4 of the Reichspräsident´s decree of 28.2.33.
The amount of the late Major Georg Konrad Kissling´s share in the business has to be reported immediately,

                                signed Dr. Scharpwinkel
                                SS-Obersturmbannführer

                                LS Certified
                                Signature
                                Kriminalinspektor

in the Western Isles he would occupy his usual room in the Lochboisdale Hotel, spending the evenings visiting or entertaining the hotel bar, and the days on trips to Eriskay to see old friends, or to the machair with younger people with whom he had struck up a relationship.

He seems, without ever having been involved in youth work or organised youth activity, to have had a natural genius for talking to young people: he is remembered warmly by many of those who grew up in South Uist, some of whom – like the MacLellan brothers – he found work for on the mainland. With his network of contacts he arranged for each of the brothers to get apprenticeships in the motor trade in the East of Scotland, despite some misgivings by their parents. And when in Edinburgh he would arrange to see them, to check how they were doing. In another age this might be the stuff of suspicion and gossip – but in the Uist of the late 1940s the biggest reservations about Kissling were his German roots. Before the war some had thought he was a spy, though what there was to spy on amongst the remote beaches and bare hills of Uist was anyone's guess. The suspicion lingered on and became folklore. Yet by the time there was something worth spying on in these islands – the rocket range at Benbecula and the well guarded radar sites in North and South Uist – it was Russia that was the enemy, not Germany.

Kissling's most important publications – his work on the black house – twice appeared in article form in *Man*, the journal of the Royal Anthropological Institute, in 1944 and 1946. He gave a copy of the first, uncorrected, proof of the latter article to Andrew Croft shortly before it was published. The sequencing of the articles gave Kissling the opportunity to develop some of his ideas about how a black house might be constructed with more modern materials in order to adapt its best qualities for contemporary use. He received some assistance in this thinking from the Building Research Station of the Department of Scientific and Industrial Research. In the latter article he included a floorplan of the ground and first floors of a 'new Hebrides House on traditional lines'.

He continued to develop these ideas on his visits in the 1940s and early 50s, whilst deploring the continuing demolition of black house after black house. But whilst his academic studies continued, he was having increasing difficulties in making sure that his mother was well looked after in Cambridge when he was away. He was also having difficulty in securing his mother's income from the property she had left behind in Germany. From 1946 until 1954 he spent £6300 on his mother's subsistence – a clinical assessment of the total that emerged in an 'Agreement' entered into by Werner and his mother in September 1954, in front of a notary public in Melrose.

This agreement – signed some time after Werner had bought the Kings Arms Hotel in Melrose – seems to conclude a period of financial uncertainty for Kissling. With the family fortune tied up in property and business in Germany, the end of the war brought little financial relief. The fact that Werner had survived so well indicates that he had private means in England, but he would have been mindful of the need for long-term finance, which could only come from the German wealth that was threatened by the cataclysm that had overtaken his family and their country. So sometime in the early 1950s Werner went to court in the American zone of his divided homeland in order to secure title to the wealth that was left.

The court case was successful for Werner, but the legacy of it was bitter – even in the 1990s there was a reserve amongst those who were left, borne of family stories of wrongs done and not righted. And in 1954 the 'Agreement' mopped up what was left – for the terms of it gifted to Werner not just the proceeds of a property sale in Wiesbaden – presumably the house that Johanna had purchased when she moved from Heizendorf – but also 'All claims appertaining to war damage, property damage, compensation etc., by whatever name described'.

Such claims were assisted by the *Lastenausgleichsgesetz*, the 'equalisation of burdens law' enacted in 1952. This taxed those who had been lucky enough to preserve all or most of their property during the war and benefited – through grants and low-interest loans – the refugees, the expelled and all others (including victims of Nazism) who had lost almost everything. Johanna Kissling had a legitimate claim under the law and would have received some recompense for what had been taken – although by no means all, as the work of her great-nephew Bolko evidenced in the early 1990s as he tried to regain some of the property that had been under Polish control for almost 50 years.

Werner's wealth in the early 1950s was enough for him to spend a modern-day fortune on shoes from Lobbs of London, regarded as the best shoemaker in the capital. He had a fixation for shoes, once baring his foot for Rosemary Croft in their home in Chelsea to show that he had no bunions or corns – the result, he claimed, of hand-made footwear. He was also wealthy enough to devise a solution to the problem his mother had created – the problem of having someone always at home, with no arrangement for care as she grew older.

In the early 1950s Kissling had noticed a number of good, solid, country hotels in Scotland and after some enquiry had discovered that the Kings Arms in Melrose was for sale. He completed the purchase in 1952 and thereafter his mother stayed in Melrose at the hotel while he travelled: a compromise she still disliked intensely, because she disliked everything about her son's adopted country. The Kings Arms, of course, was meant to be more than a convenient home for his mother: it was a business that would put to work the money he still had, and make it grow. But Werner was no businessman.

At first the hotel appeared to flourish: he introduced pony-trekking – virtually unknown in Scotland – and staffed the hotel to cope with the best and most discriminating of trade. The Kings Arms, as an old coaching inn, had plenty of space and outbuildings to spare and Werner filled up what was

JOHANNA KISSLING IN THE KINGS ARMS HOTEL, MELROSE

SHORTLY BEFORE HER DEATH IN 1961.

Pony Trekking
and
Trail Riding
in the
Scottish Borders

King's Arms Hotel

MELROSE

Roxburghshire

Telephone 113

A.A.   R.A.C.

BROCHURE FOR THE KINGS ARMS HOTEL, MELROSE, WHICH WERNER
KISSLING OWNED DURING THE FIFTIES AND SIXTIES.

available with those who would run the place according to his exacting standards – when he was present.

But he was not present nearly enough. All through the 50s the trips continued – to Uist, to Eriskay, across the Borders to Dumfries (where the architecture and the traditional crafts of the Solway attracted his interest) to the West Riding of Yorkshire again to record crafts and dying customs. He also travelled to other places to call on friends and research items that caught his attention. Publication was irregular, and mostly in specialist journals, but it was the pursuit and recording of such knowledge that mattered to Werner. It was not an activity designed to make money, though he would shortly have to turn it to that purpose.

Meanwhile the hotel was under management: and almost from the outset a Mr Lawson came to manage the establishment which Werner often used as his own home for entertaining and for welcoming guests as distinguished as Calum I MacLean, the folklorist and brother of the Gaelic poet, Sorley MacLean.

These evenings when guests were staying – at Werner's expense, and thus at no profit to the hotel – were lively and stimulating: discussions of traditional ways of life, of housing, of crafts and traditions would give way to drinking sessions in the bar and the lilt of Gaelic songs. For someone who had spent so long immersed in the Gaelic world of Eriskay and South Uist – truly part of the Gaelic heartland – Werner had little, if any knowledge of the language. But he enjoyed hearing it sung or recited as it would be on those evenings in Melrose. And he enjoyed – increasingly – the drams that would be sunk again and again as the night progressed.

For most of the 1950s Werner enjoyed the life of a gentleman hotel proprietor in Melrose – concerning himself as little as possible with the details of the business (as long as appearances were kept up) and absent for long periods pursuing his interests. These might mean a week in the Yorkshire Dales photographing the last cheesemaker, then a month in South Uist and a journey back via Oban and Edinburgh. They certainly did not include keeping a close eye on the business, even though its progress was taking several turns for the worse.

Lawson remained manager, and his relationship with Kissling was sufficiently close for Werner to accept the honour of being named godfather to a son, Christopher, christened in the Episcopal Church in Melrose on July 19, 1954, and sufficiently close for Werner to keep the certificate of baptism in his suitcase until he died.

However, under Lawson the hotel's financial position worsened with each succeeding year. Werner was regularly putting more money into the business to stave off financial failure but although – as Peter MacLellan put it – he had 'a good place there', nothing seemed to work. Some, including Werner, blamed Lawson although lack of supervision may well have been the root cause.

Then, in 1961, his beloved mother died: unhappy to the last and still regretting the loss of those spacious days at Heizendorf.

During the 1960s the hotel staggered on, showing more and more a lack of management and expertise. Financial collapse, never far away, eventually arrived. From a position of relative security and wealth, Kissling found himself literally flat broke.

The hotel had drained away his fortune and with no more available from his mother (the 'Agreement' had given him her estate and fortune some seven years before her death) he faced old age as the financial antithesis of his youth and expensive middle years. Even his Lobb's account was closed, with the plaintive words 'Gone away' written across the last entry in the ledger – an entry that records the sum of one shilling and sixpence still owing.

By then aged over 70, he was also homeless. His life as a gentleman was over and all he had to fall back on was his camera and his scholarship, both of which were products of a different age. The Borders town of Dumfries seemed as good a place as any to start the final years, and that is where Werner found himself, in a small, sparse, rented flat with nothing to his name except his memories, his suitcase and a thirst for knowledge that was stronger than ever.

KISSLING, SIX MONTHS BEFORE HIS DEATH IN 1988. THE PHOTOGRAPH
HAS A SPIDERY INSCRIPTION IN GERMAN ON THE REVERSE AND SEEMS
TO HAVE BEEN INTENDED FOR HIS FAMILY.

CHAPTER 9

Final Years

Kissling appeared to choose Dumfries for no better reason than he had enjoyed taking photographs there in the 1950s and 1960s and admired the buildings and the access to the many extant traditional crafts that still existed along the Solway and in Galloway. In 1968, at the age of 73, he settled in the town and it was there that he stayed until his death in 1988. His small flat, just across from the Dumfries Museum, was rented and provided little more than a place to lay his head. With his Leica and his aristocratic bearing he would soon become a regular visitor to the museum, researching crafts and asking questions of the staff and the curator, Alf Truckle, one of Scotland's most distinguished local historians.

From the mid-60s on he had begun to show a concern for money and had started to seek money to pay for his research trips to the Yorkshire Dales and across the Scottish Borders. But his wealth of contacts from the pre- and post-war years were themselves dead or had moved on. Edinburgh University's School of Scottish Studies paid a little for information and photographs: Leeds University and some other academic establishments would provide some money but not regularly, and not for ever. In an age where conventional scholarship was giving way to revisionism, there was a limited interest in the purchase of meticulous hand-written sheets with small mounted photographs, and careful annotations of the nuances of traditional crafts.

But Kissling the observer retained his skill and scrupulous attention to detail. In the basement of Dumfries Museum there are several boxes of carefully arranged materials, investigating local activities as diverse as cheesemaking, salmon netting, barrel manufacture, rope twining and many other domestic industries that would never be seen again.

He also submitted articles and photographs to magazines and had intermittent success -- an article on Southerness lighthouse in *Scotland's*

Magazine in 1958 seems to be the first and further articles followed over the next few years (in that publication and in the *Scots Magazine*) on drystane dyking, Solway fishing, and the grinding of corn in a quern. Some of his photographs illustrated other articles, including those in academic journals such as *Scottish Studies*.[1]

He also continued to write and research longer pieces from which shorter articles were taken. One of these is on 'Witchcraft in Galloway', a subject off the usual track of Werner's practical, ethnological mind.

Unusually for a man who had spent so long being a photographer, Kissling never developed his own prints, always having them done by a London firm until financial stringency required him to seek developing from the cheapest source. But Boots did not take instructions about how to produce finished prints, and the need for the utmost care in exposure and Kissling's frustration with lowering standards made him less and less satisfied

HAAF NETTING FOR SALMON IN THE NITH ESTUARY. TAKEN BY KISSLING FOR DUMFRIES MUSEUM IN THE 1960s.

---

[1] The publication of the School of Scottish Studies to which Werner had sold and given a large number of prints of the Hebrides, the originals of which are usually to be found in his lantern slide collection or in the boxes of negatives in Dumfries Museum.

A SHEET OF ANNOTATED CONTACT PRINTS, TYPICAL OF THE MANY HUNDREDS
OF SUCH SHEETS KISSLING PREPARED FOR HIS ETHNOLOGICAL STUDIES. THESE
PICTURES EXAMINE BUTTER-MAKING IN THE WEST RIDING OF
YORKSHIRE SOME TIME IN THE 1960s.

with what his ancient Leica could produce.

He retained a talent, though, for talking to and learning from ordinary people. Dumfries became used to the distinguished, grey-haired émigré in its midst, and he would take regular trips out into the Galloway countryside, often returning with examples of farm implements that were long disused –or with information about where they could be had for the asking.

Kissling's first days at the museum were not easy for either himself or for those who worked there. The distinguished stranger knew more than they, and with his easy learning and his ability to talk of figures from history with intimate knowledge – figures as diverse as Ramsay MacDonald and Adolf Hitler – some thought that he was an imposter or fantasist. There was also an edge of professional jealousy: an academic with languages and a familiarity with the details of ethnology threatened the small empires of learning that arise in any small town. Dumfries took time to absorb him.

Kissling's bitterness about his reduced circumstances did not show through to those who he got to know in Dumfries. He usually had the price of a whisky in one of the local pubs, and was a regular in several, but his feelings do emerge in what little of his correspondence still survives. He had tax problems that lingered from his failed hotel and he seems to have been poor at dealing with the minutiae of officialdom. His state pension was a constant source of difficulty – even in his mid-seventies he had virtually no documentation of his past employment!

He sold the odd photograph when he could, often selling the same one to several different museums or academic departments and he had one or two friends who provided some additional financial support. He would be tirelessly grateful for assistance, although his correspondence reveals a constant embarrassment about his position. David Lockwood claims that he never had difficulty in talking about, or taking, money and had a casual attitude to it. But that hid a sense of failure and disappointment that for the first time in his life, he had to think about, and experience, the reality of being constantly in debt without any knowledge of where money for even the barest essentials was to come from. On top of this, Werner was also beginning to suffer from ill health.

In the late 1970s – just at the time when the Scottish Film Archive were given *A Poem of Remote Lives* by the School of Scottish Studies, which had received a print of it from Werner in the 1950s – he was taken to hospital with pneumonia, and although he returned to his flat after a period in hospital, his health deteriorated during the 1980s.

In the autumn of 1978 Dumfries Museum mounted an exhibition of Kissling's photographs, as a 'retrospective' tribute to the 83 year old who was now something of a local legend. Alf Truckle contributed the introduction to the sketchy, cyclostyled catalogue, but the descriptions are by Werner himself.

The first 12 photographs (or sets of prints – some items have as many

as eight individual pictures) are from the Western Isles, the next seven from New Zealand and the remaining 14 show Scottish crafts or artefacts. The final print in the exhibition is a photograph of Kissling himself, with a fuller face than that of his early years, but looking much less than his age. This photograph is by 'my good friend David Lockwood' as Kissling puts it. David Lockwood came to Dumfries Museum in the late 70s and took over as curator shortly afterwards, when Alf Truckle retired. With the job came Dr Kissling – a figure constantly in the museum, constantly researching, writing or offering material. Truckle had secured a small honorarium for Kissling so that he could be attached to the museum staff as a collector and codifier of traditional material and the collection of rural implements had burgeoned under his eye. Restored rooms in the tower leading to the museum's camera obscura are now lined with a eclectic collection of items that speak of a time long past.

Lockwood was young, eager and interested and he struck up an immediate rapport with Kissling. Werner was used to an audience, and had found one in the pubs of Dumfries as well as in the local antiquarian society where he made a firm friendship with Ralph Coleman to whom he told stories of his life in Germany and revealed his strong fear of the police. It was to Coleman that he related the details of his encounters with the Gestapo, and to whom he told yet another version of his supposed arrest at the German Embassy in 1933 – an arrest which, as we have seen, could not have happened in the way Werner suggested. And it was to Coleman that he recited the story of meeting the Nazi functionaries in the Reichstag as they waited to see Stresemann during the Beer Hall Putsch.

But it was to Lockwood that Kissling began to talk of his real achievements – his time in Eriskay and the work he had done at Cambridge. And as Lockwood was shown his photographs and the original lantern slides, still in their wooden cases, the two of them talked about getting a wider audience again for the tremendous images that had been neglected for so long. It was Lockwood who was the driving force behind the exhibition and it was he who was to make sure that Kissling was not forgotten.

His failing health meant that he was less and less mobile, but he still managed to attend the museum regularly and to build the friendships with the staff and visitors who meant so much to him. The museum held a further exhibition in 1983 and, in a letter to Andrew Croft, he spoke enthusiastically about it. However, he was somewhat dismissive of a wildly inaccurate report in the local paper headed 'Brilliant Work Of County Nazi Victim Goes On Display' which, amongst other errors, claimed that the Nazis had hanged his brother, killed his father and imprisoned his mother! 'The article brought many people to the Museum and to me here, now at home in the flat. I think that the calibre . . . of the writer of the article in Dumfries (!) is . . . provincial and rather touchingly so', he told Croft.

WERNER KISSLING AT THE OPENING OF AN EXHIBITION OF
HIS WORK IN DUMFRIES IN 1978.

He also maintained some other correspondence, but it was Andrew and Rosalind Croft who were the most regular of those who kept in touch with him. They also visited him in Dumfries on at least one occasion and sent him money and gifts – including a music centre which David Lockwood bought on their behalf and erected in the tiny flat, to Werner's delight. But Werner's letters were becoming almost illegible by the early 80s, although surprisingly the handwriting recovered somewhat in the two years before he died. He had also made a number of newer friends, including a young American, Craig Meyer, who, when back at home in America, corresponded regularly with Werner and purchased his photographs, the sales of which were more than welcome.

In addition to lung problems, Werner suffered from arthritis and received treatment in Edinburgh for a while. He moved from his flat to a local nursing home and alternated between the two for the remainder of his life. One of his letters to Andrew Croft speaks in frustration of the 'pompous little men' from the DSS who arranged sheltered housing for him in 1986. Some years before he had asked David Lockwood if he should sell his camera (he had received an offer for it in a pub) and Lockwood had agreed that if he could no longer use it, then it should go. His last photographs were taken when he was in his late eighties – a photographic career that had started in Riga in 1919 came to an end over 60 years later in Dumfries.

The exhibitions of 1978 and 1983 produced a flurry of interest in Werner Kissling and his life with a number of local articles published which portrayed a romanticised version of his life and which seemed to create a legend of their own. At least one television company expressed an interest in making a documentary about him, but he told his Dumfries friends that he did not want publicity and would not encourage it. The television proposal went no further. As Dumfries Museum was developed to serve the whole of the Dumfries and Galloway region, not just the town, Werner was still keen at the age of 92 to be involved in the process: 'It is my hope', he observes in another letter to Andrew Croft, 'that I will be fit enough to help putting what was my concern in reasonable order and, I trust, in David's care'.

But it was not to be. In the same letter – dated August 1987 – he tells the Crofts that he has had a fall again – 'wholly due to my misting eyesight' – and by the end of that year he was permanently resident in Moorheads Nursing Home, where he longed for visitors and enjoyed himself hugely when they came.

Naturally, David Lockwood was a regular, and in late January 1988 Werner appointed him his executor, entrusting to him what little money was left as well as the suitcase of papers and photographs and the two wooden boxes of lantern slides. By now Werner was fading fast although he seemed in remarkably little pain or discomfort.

A few days after he had made his will, David Lockwood, his girlfriend (and later wife) Jennifer and two friends spent the evening with Werner in his little room in Moorheads. 'Werner', wrote David in a letter to Andrew Croft, 'was never brighter and loved all the excitement – at one stage he had three drinks on the go at the same time – whisky, tea and water! This night is the one I think about. The memory will stay for a long time. The next day he was dozy again and he died at about one in the morning'.

Werner Kissling died in Moorheads Nursing Home in Dumfries on the 3rd of February 1988 – just two months short of his 93rd birthday. Two days later an obituary in *The Times* spoke of him as 'a man of high principle, intense idealism and great sensitivity . . . with a gift for friendship' and the tone and terms of the notice make one suspect that it was written by the ever-faithful Andrew Croft. Smaller, derivative obituaries appeared in the *Daily Telegraph* ('Hitler's arrest secretary dies') and the *Independent. The Scotsman* also had a Gaelic comment on his death in the regular Saturday Gaelic column.

The estate contained virtually no money, barely enough for David to pay for the funeral. The burial plot in St Michael's Kirkyard belonged to Moorheads home and was therefore owned by the district council. It was what would have been called in former days a 'pauper's grave'. There were no funds left to pay for a headstone, but David Lockwood and the Dumfries antiquarian society launched an appeal in the autumn of 1989 in order to raise £500 for that task, and the sum was quickly realised.

Two years to the day after his death an unveiling ceremony took place at Kissling's graveside. It also received newspaper coverage, and to this day a single red rose is placed on the grave regularly, but by whom no one knows.

'A mystery right enough', as one of the MacLellan brothers said in the film that I finally made about Kissling, some seven years after his death.

DETAIL OF AN ERISKAY BLACK HOUSE, 1934.

CHAPTER 10

Eriskay Revisited

These days the yachts that sail into Eriskay in the summer are unlikely to bring ethnologists or cultural recorders and more likely to contain tourists for whom a sail in the Hebrides carries a more welcome risk and variation of weather than a flotilla holiday in the Aegean. Landing at Acairsaid Mhor a tarmacadam road leads over to Haun -- but that way is more travelled in the opposite direction, with those visiting on the car ferry from South Uist and walking, biking or even driving to the harbour and to the few fishing boats that still seek out lobsters around the shores of Uist and Barra.

Eriskay's population has plummeted since Kissling's visit. His '470 people', for whom he wanted running water and some of the comforts of modern life declined to almost below 100 in the 70s although numbers rose again in the 80s as mainland unemployment reduced the charms or the inevitability of emigration. Comparing Eriskay today to the Eriskay that Kissling observed and recorded there are a number of curious similarities that lie alongside the striking differences.

The landscape is the same, providing one's eyes can rise above or away from the proliferation of modern housing. Barra still lies in brooding shadow to the south-west, and a sparkling summer day on the Prince's Strand is backdropped by the same amazing expanse of ocean and island that draws the eye and urges any feeling individual onto the water and away towards the horizon.

To the north the hills of South Uist seem to close in the Sound of Eriskay, underneath which lies the wreck of the SS *Politician*, with some of its cargo of bicycles, cotton print dresses and – of course – whisky still trapped in the shifting sandbanks that brought that now famous vessel to its ruin. I doubt if its end was half as romantic as the moment when Compton MacKenzie himself, playing the role of captain of the SS *Cabinet Minister* in the film of his book, *Whisky Galore*, shouts into the fog: 'Hark – isn't that the bell on the Skerry Mhor?' Just after he utters the words, the ship strikes the rocks and the film cuts to the islanders of Todday who realise that the ship's fog horn has stopped and that must mean there is a wreck to be found, whose appropriate riches for the whisky-starved island are yet to be guessed at!

It is that fictionalised account of a real event that gives Eriskay most of its fame today. The local pub – opened by the enterprising television producer Allan MacDonald whose father knew Kissling and who visited him in Dumfries in the last years of Kissling's life – is called 'The Politician' and displays behind the bar the inevitable empty bottle from the cargo of the sort that a hundred families keep in Uist. One of these was first shown to me by Donald MacAulay of the Creagorry Hotel in Benbecula where, as a fresh-faced incomer, I used to drink every night after work. I was also lucky enough to be able to celebrate this remarkable, historic hotel in a television documentary, *Creagoraidh*, made in the hot summer of 1991.

Preparing the Kissling documentary, I had the idea of taking some of the original photographs back to Eriskay and involving the community in identifying those who had been recorded in 1934. Trapped in Edinburgh by one of the recurring political excitements that are my lot, it fell to Ishbel MacIver and Flora Thomson to arrange the filming on Eriskay and to take the crew and a set of 35mm copies of the lantern slides to Eriskay for a community ceilidh. This was arranged with the help of the formidable Fr Callum MacLellan, parish priest of the island and former Vice-Convenor of Comhairle Nan Eilean (the Western Isles Islands Council) which started in 1974 with such high hopes and vision, but which by 1990 had degenerated into incompetence and farce.[1]

Both the ceilidh and the resulting footage were outstanding successes. On camera the whole of the island became involved in identifying places and people, and one or two individuals were confronted by images of themselves and their families as they were 60 years ago. There were also memories of Kissling, of the yacht, the Skyeman who was the skipper and of the three Germans who were there with Kissling for at least part of the time. And also

---

[1] The council invested £27 million of ratepayers' money in the Bank of Credit and Commerce International which subsequently crashed. I investigated the background to this story in a 50-minute STV special investigation transmitted in January 1992.

memories of Kissling's later visits, including showing the slides at school some time after the war.

Rathad Kissling[2] is still to be seen on Eriskay – the stretch of road over to the harbour which was built with the money from the film première in London, although only the oldest of those present still knew it by that name. For the younger ones present it was also an opportunity to see a very different island. For much of what Kissling had sought in terms of progress has been achieved over the years, although it has swept away the majority of what he regarded as the traditional strengths of the place.

It is perhaps easiest to quantify those differences by returning to the film itself and to the aspects of traditional life that he covered. At the end of chapter four I summarised the film thus:

"*The film starts with a 'placing' of the island and some sketchy information on its most famous moment in history – the landing of Charles Edward Stuart in 1744. It then briefly looks at agriculture and peat cutting and by way of explanation of the poor soil leads into an examination of the 'sheep-based' industries that the people are involved in, with some sideways glances at fishing as an occupation. It concludes by tying together the domestic life of the people with their culture and concludes on the note of romanticism with which it began.*"

Certainly the island is probably less known today than it was in 1934, although *Whisky Galore* has ensured some additional notoriety, even amongst the audiences that know the film as *Tight Little Island* (in North America) and *Whisky A Go-Go* (in France).

With no hotel, though some small availability of bed and breakfast, tourism is still a patchy matter, though people do come across on the car ferry and spend a few hours walking the island or even travelling the limited number of roads in their cars which they have ferried over at considerable expense. The island pub provides refuge for them, and there is the church to visit, on its rocky point above Haun and with a unique altar (half of a lifeboat bow from HMS *Hermes*) and its bell from the German battle cruiser *Derfflinger*, scuttled in Scapa Flow.

The church indeed looks little different from the shot of it in the GPO Film Unit 1939 production *Islanders*, and although the mail to Eriskay now comes even more reliably and speedily than in 1939, the Post Office and its services remain of vital importance to the small community. Not just because, in Auden's words from *Night Mail*, 'Who can bear to think themselves forgotten?' (and there is always the fear of being forgotten on a small island the Government regularly passes by), but also because shopping by post – another service commented on in *Islanders* – remains a mainstay of island life.

In the early summer the pink sea convolvulus (*Calystegia soldanella*) can be found on the shore above the Prince's Strand, its heart shaped leaf and large

2 Kissling's Road

trumpet making a striking splash of colour. It was once believed that the plant only grew on Eriskay, and had grown from seeds dropped by the Prince when he landed, but in fact it is found on other Hebridean islands, most notably Vatersay to the south of Barra.

The poverty of the island soil, remarked upon by Kissling, was paradoxically the reason why the island retained most of the population and increased in the 19th century when the Clanranald estates had been sold to General Gordon of Cluny. Whilst clearing South Uist and parts of Barra, he permitted the Eriskay people to remain and for some from Uist to join them because he did not believe that the island would support them for very long.

Agriculture is now even less in existence than it was when Kissling visited. The island crofts can support sheep but little else, and no corn is now grown. In any case the amount of land throughout Uist under cultivation has diminished considerably in the last 60 years as more intensive methods of farming made smaller, labour-intensive patches less and less attractive or viable. Some potatoes are grown, but only for domestic use.

Peat cutting is also going out of fashion. The best peat banks have long since been exhausted and the ease of obtaining coal, or even gas or oil for central heating has lead to fewer people being bothered with the process of turfing, cutting, drying and transporting – particularly as Eriskay ponies are now scarce, and nothing better exists with which to haul the peat home. Peat cutting machines, becoming more common elsewhere, are not well suited for rocky areas and would be difficult to use in areas as distant from good roads as the Eriskay peat banks.

Sheep, however, are still part of the Eriskay landscape. They are no doubt fewer in number, but the process of gathering, dipping and dosing them is essentially the same, even if the odd quad bike has speeded up some of the routine, and the dipping and dosing are more scientific. Shearing is faster too with electric clippers, although some of the old sort still survive.

But the arts of dying, carding, spinning and the *luadh* are gone completely – as has the local weaving. And even the traditional knitting is done with imported wool – more cost effective, and presumably more quality controlled.

Fishing has also changed utterly – all that is left is some lobster and prawn fishing and the days of the steam-driven line trawlers are gone forever. The herring and mackerel caught is for domestic consumption or, more probably, to bait the lobster creels before they are laid in the shallow waters around the island.

Looking out across those waters are a new generation of houses – in fact several new generations. The black houses were becoming a thing of the past even in Kissling's time: the new houses of the type that Kissling lodged in were being built by the end of the 19th century, and they were developed and refined up until the Second World War. After the war bungalows became

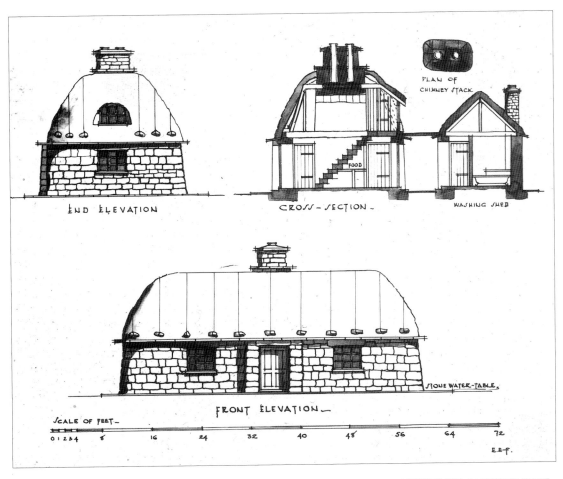

END ELEVATION

CROSS-SECTION

PLAN OF CHIMNEY STACK

FOOD

WASHING SHED

FRONT ELEVATION

STONE WATER-TABLE

SCALE OF FEET

0 1 2 3 4   8   16   24   32   40   48   56   64   72

E.B.F.

THESE METICULOUS ELEVATIONS OF A TWO-STOREY BLACK HOUSE FROM KISSLING'S LANTERN SLIDE
COLLECTION BETRAY HIS ADMIRATION FOR A TYPE OF HABITATION WHICH HE CONSIDERED IDEAL
FOR THE HEBRIDEAN ENVIRONMENT.

more popular due to lower building cost and a lower profile to the prevailing, buffeting, westerly wind. And modern bungalows are still being built, aided by the grant and loan schemes that are available to crofting families. Visitors to the islands are constantly struck by the profusion of these, often large, modern homes which are, in places, a replacement for the draughty caravans which were temporary shelters for many young families just starting out in the sixties and early seventies. But they are also a feature of life in western Ireland, where there is greater prosperity and still the urge to build on the land and make it one's own.

The school still operates but with far fewer pupils – those of year three and above in the secondary can now go to Uist, although primary education is still available and – almost uniquely in Scotland – the first couple of years of secondary. The school got its water supply, and much else besides. Now teachers visit from Uist for a variety of subjects and computer links give the pupils a gateway on the world which Kissling could never have imagined.

The telephone has changed the whole of the Western Isles, as has better road and ferry links and regular air transport. Today you can get to Eriskay from Glasgow in less than three hours: one hour to fly to Benbecula, half an hour to allow the collection of luggage and a car, another hour to get to Ludag and the car ferry and the last half hour or thereabouts to cross to Haun and your destination, providing the tide is right. The shoals and sandbanks of the sound still prevent a crossing at low water so nature is still able to assert itself in human plans at least twice a day.

Accessibility works the other way as well. Those living on Eriskay who were dependent upon the occasional trip to a general store in South Uist – if that, for normally they would rely on goods sent to the island and the visits of itinerant peddlers[3] – can now drive for their weekend shopping to the army NAAFI in Benbecula (the only one open to the general public) and to a variety of other shops (including an excellent bakery) in and around Balivanich, now the *de facto* capital of the southern isles.

Gaelic is still the predominant language of the whole of the Western Isles, but certainly there is more English to be heard, even on Eriskay, than would have been the case during Kissling's visits. A combination of the effects of incomers, constant emigration and return and radio and television have all taken their toll, although in recent years an increase in both Gaelic media and Gaelic education has endeavoured to assist the survival of the language which was threatened with complete disappearance in the sixties. A mixture of English and Gaelic can still be heard in the playground, in the pubs and in the shops with English often predominating. But Gaelic remains the language of home although not necessarily all the time, and not when television

dominates. With no single Gaelic channel as yet Gaelic programming is still at the mercy of schedules dictated from far away.

The somewhat fragile nature of the Gaelic community in Eriskay and elsewhere is often commented upon by those who visit the islands from Ireland. Despite a far from perfect situation in the Irish Gaeltachds, the situation there allows Gaelic to be used much more as the language of the living community. The work done by Irish folklore collectors in Eriskay when Kissling was visiting seems to have informed, after many false starts and wrong turnings, a more committed attitude at national level to the importance of the language. Perhaps the legal status afforded to the Irish language has made all the difference – a legal status still denied to the Gael, incredible as that may seem, at end of the twentieth century. And that change in the underpinning of the community may explain the final difference that Kissling might observe were he to see his beloved island today. For in his film it is the community nature of work that is stressed, and the way in which individual effort is dovetailed into the good of the whole.

Such communality is less in evidence in the Western Isles and in Eriskay today. The informal ceilidh has all but ended and although doors are left open (in most places) and visits are made without forewarning or ceremony, there are fewer and fewer parts of the yearly round that require the community to work together, and less need for individuals to give of their labour to help the general good.

And if there are less formal occasions, then there are also less informal occasions – gatherings after the work is done at which stories are told and songs sung. Such occasions do take place in the community hall, but they are an adjunct of something else – a dance or even a showing of slides, such as the one that was organised in the early autumn of 1995 in order to recall a visitor on a yacht well over half a century ago.

It may not have been as I described it earlier 'tying together the domestic life of the people with their culture and conclud(ing) on the note of romanticism' but it was a joyful event all the same. And the romanticism of Kissling (or of his editor) was never much of an aspect of the daily life of the ordinary people of any of the Western Isles – it was an import like many other, used to excuse the generations of outside neglect and cultural theft that typified, and still perhaps today typify, the relationship of the 'Gall' with the 'Gael'. Romanticism sells, after all, and few if any of the consumers would be able to go and see the harsh reality upon which it was founded.

Yet that harsh reality is not so sharp-edged today. The price that has been paid for more comfort, better housing and better communications is, however, a softening else of the distinctness of the community. It was, after all, contact and the development of dependency that led to the evacuation of St Kilda, not remoteness and isolation. Contact and dependency on what all of us take for granted – television, frozen food, daily newspapers and foreign

---

[3] As late as the 1970s a ubiquitous brown paper package for one resident regularly arrived, said to contain books, but always chinking suspiciously. One day it was leaking whisky after it was dropped 'by accident'.

holidays to name but a few of the 'drugs' – has been the inevitable by-product of the last half century's technological progress. In different forms it will have the same effect in the next 50 years. And it comes from human ambition, not from weakness or greed.

And in another half century the Eriskay that I remember from visits to show films in the late 70s and from a trip to video a school play and outing in 1979 (during which the supervising teacher and I started a courting that was to lead to marriage a year later) will, I suspect, have changed as utterly again. Again because of ambition, and the relentless drive of all the people in all parts of the world to join in and take part in the good things that are danced before our eyes day in and day out.

That's progress and not all the ethnology in the world will hold it back. Though those who practice that discipline can use it to at least record what has passed. And Kissling was a fine recorder.

CHAPTER 11

Enigma and Legacy

In the past three years I have found out more about Werner Kissling than, I suspect, many of his friends ever knew. And yet when I came to choose a title for the documentary and for this book, the word 'enigma' still seemed entirely apposite.

Yet at least one of the questions that had arisen on that first evening when I saw his film, and walked along the beach at Ardivachar discussing it, is easy to answer. His interest in the Western Isles arose from his mother's trip, and a relic of that, in the shape of her postcard, had been in his possession for most of his life. It perhaps also awakened his interest in ethnology and the two inheritances worked well together. For a man looking for a cause or an interest to absorb him, it was as good as any other and as well or deliberately chosen, I suspect, as any of our life decisions are.

Yet that choice or destiny has had many effects. For example today on the Isle of Skye two young architects are involved in re-creating the traditional black house design for modern domestic use. Dualchas[1] Building Design, the brainchild of Alasdair and Neil Steafan, is developing high quality modern housing – ideally suited for, and much needed by the Western Isles – which is firmly based not just on the traditional black house, but also firmly on Kissling's own ideas about how such housing could be made suitable for continued occupation. Their success, and that of others who may imitate them, would glorify the landscape of the islands once again with buildings that suit it – which many of the modern bungalows do not.

Alasdair and Neil put it well in their own promotional literature, calling an tigh dubh[2] 'the only true vernacular architecture of Gaelic Scotland' and going on to comment that 'the form is based on the traditional long house allowing the building to be slotted into the shape of the land, not to sit clumsily in the landscape as most modern kit houses do'. They praise the energy efficiency of the black house, whilst pointing out that timber-stud construction can be easily adapted to the black house shape, with extra expense only required in the stone cladding – which is in itself a magnificent form of additional insulation. Kissling knew and wrote about that half a century ago.

And Kissling's film on Eriskay – now more than 60 years old – is constantly in use in documentary and reportage, often without a formal acknowledgement on screen. It is thus that his eye and his vision informs much of our own language of images of the recent Hebridean past.

His photographs are increasingly seen on book covers, or in the steady spawn of books on Scotland and its rural past and modern photographers pay homage to the way in which he observed. Calum Angus Mackay, one of the best new Scottish photographers, says that 'Kissling's photographs are on a par with George Washington Wilson and Margaret Fay Shaw and perhaps even Paul Strand. Strand was a professional photographer and he was taking photographs for sale all over the world: Margaret Fay Shaw quite often took photographs relating to folklore, history and songs and George Washington Wilson was primarily a topographical photographer. But Kissling took pictures of people and their way of life – that's what he recorded and he did not have people posing for him. He was trying to make them as natural as possible.'[3]

The ability to touch ordinary people and tell something about them is also attractive to Allan MacDonald, who says: 'To me, as an Eriskay man, they are interesting because I am looking beyond the outer layer of the photograph. I am making a spiritual connection to the people who have gone when I look at Kissling's photographs and I see the lines on their faces, what is in their eyes, what they are telling me about their way of life.'[4]

Kissling himself summarised his own achievements thus: 'I have had the good fortune to live with the people of the Western Isles a good many years ago, before the most important changes affecting the rural scene had taken place and so be able to record the old ways.'

---

[1] Traditional
[2] The Black House

[3 & 4] Transcriptions from Eala Bhan documentary *Kissling Duin'Iom'Fhillte* (1996) for BBC Alba, funded by CTG

A modest enough assessment – but he went on to say something more profound that gives a substantial clue to his character. He added: 'Everywhere today new houses are being built to uniform specifications: the black house has disappeared – not necessarily a matter for regret – but with it has disappeared many a ceilidh and by degrees the desire for spontaneous self-expression by the people, be it in song and poetry, the making of tools or the dying of home-made tweeds. Can they – and can we – do without it?'

When I first started to research the life and work Werner Kissling, I felt myself confronted with a succession of stereotypes: the Prussian officer, the aristocratic diplomat, the amateur academic, the rich dilettante, and finally the impoverished but proud old man, full of memories. But in time these have resolved themselves into merely outward signs of a much more sensitive personality – and one which was devoted to 'spontaneous self-expression'. It is this lifelong desire to be free of restriction that really provides the clue to the enigmas that surround Kissling.

The first of these is the enigma of his background and breeding. There is no doubt that Kissling found the formalised rituals of his childhood irksome and his family background constricting. So too, I believe, did his mother who revelled in the long trips abroad and in her photography. They were the like minds of the Kissling family, and were fortunate in being able to use the family wealth to support their wishes and interests – particularly after Werner's father died. It was also her money that allowed him the freedom of the years before her death. She in turn became free when she left Germany, although she came to hate her newly adopted land, perhaps because Werner enjoyed it too much and used the hotel in Melrose as a well-appointed nursing home for her, allowing him to travel at will.

But restricted as he was by this upbringing, he seemed also to have a degree of pride in it, as if it informed part of him that he valued, as well as irritating and eroding part of him that he needed.

The second is the enigma of his diplomatic career and subsequent work. His life as a diplomat only lasted for less than 13 years, and ended with resignation, not heroic expulsion as he suggested to his friends. It, too, was constricting, although it allowed him to travel and to mix in the wealthy and privileged society he enjoyed. When he was financially able to leave – again after his father's death – he did so, choosing the leisured lifestyle of a freelance academic which gave full reign to his enthusiasms with few if any restrictions – a lifestyle that allowed 'spontaneous self-expression'. And accordingly most things were one-offs: his film, which never became the larger canvas he dreamed of; his photographs which never seem to settle in one place for long; his hotel, which was a means to personal freedom; his collecting for Dumfries Museum (the activity par excellence for a dilettante – acquiring with someone else's funds, when necessary) his work on the black house, which resulted in two articles and not the doctorate he originally intended to

pursue. For a man of patient and disciplined training, he lacked internal self-discipline and the ability to finish what he had started.

The third is the enigma of his personal life. He collected friends and acquaintances some of whom, like Andrew Croft, were remarkably loyal and generous, particularly in his later years. Even at the end of his life, his good humour, intelligence and wit attracted able younger people like David Lockwood and Craig Meyer. His self-contained confidence – which sometimes only just stopped short of arrogance – meant that people again and again talk of being 'privileged' to be his friends. His stories and recollections – enhanced certainly from time to time – were fluent and gave a glimpse of another life and another age. But he was not condescending and could communicate effectively and with younger people like the MacLellan brothers who were products of a very different society.

Yet one gets little indication throughout his life of warmth and intimacy. Even his closest friends seem to be just that and no more – and apart from the unidentified young men in the photographs in his suitcase, there is no debris of lovers or romantic entanglements, no letters, no reminiscences. Perhaps this is a product of the attitude of a different time towards homosexuality, but also perhaps another aspect of his need for spontaneous self-expression – no ties, and no commitments. And that lack of ties applies also to his friendships – for they seem so often to be almost one-sided, with the effort being expended by the friends and not by Werner: until he needed something or someone.

All these are parts of the larger enigma – the enigma of his personality and motivations. There is no doubt that he was generous with money and his time – but selfish and self-centred people can be generous. It is a form of Hobbism – a means of enhancing personal satisfaction by playing out the part that generosity demands. And of course one can be selfish and self-centred with things other than money and time. There is no doubt that he was confident – but confident people can be a mass of internal doubts and conflicts which are never seen by any but the closest confidante. And if one has no close confidantes, then they are never seen and may only be surmised.

Werner Kissling was, for all but the last 20 years of his life, a lucky man. He was talented, rich, attractive and able. He was popular and sociable. In the First World War he escaped death and served out most of his time in uniform distant from the horror of the trenches. In the Second World War he had what was called a 'cushy billet' even as an internee, and was free to resume his chosen lifestyle by 1943. Even in the straitened circumstances of his last years he was able to earn a small living and was well treated by almost everyone he knew. His one stroke of really bad luck was the collapse of his hotel, and that might be traced to inaction, bad judgement and an excess of trust (a trust placed because the hotel was simply an adjunct to his lifestyle and the underpinning of it because it put the care of his mother into other hands).

But that luck was used almost entirely to make his life what he wanted. He had no obligations and seems to have had little desire to fulfil at any personal inconvenience even those he did have. It is a life that those encumbered with endless pressures on their time and on their energy – pressures often not looked for and sometimes unwelcome – can only envy. And that means most of us would envy him, although also perhaps pass some judgement on an individual and a time which allowed such freedom. Something about 'the many and the few' would seem to be an appropriate, if glib, phrase for our age.

Yet it was this very freedom that allowed him to achieve; but not in a uniform manner, or spectacularly, for that was not in his nature, and not within the confines of 'spontaneous expression'. Discipline and form are still required for achievement of that nature. But his freedom brought to bear flashes of genius in three particular areas of his life – and is so doing still sheds illumination some 60 years later.

The first of these areas is in photography. The photographs in this book illustrate this genius: an ability to capture people as they were and to let light and shade provide the additional message that seems to get beneath the skin, or into a landscape. Observers of great ability cancel out themselves, like great accompanists. Kissling's very lack of personal, one to one, emotional involvement allowed him to appreciate the nuances of character and expression and to catch them on camera. His abstract concerns for the welfare of Eriskay – and his importuning of the great and the good to improve social conditions – are Hobbism too: they were what was expected of the benefactor, and he performed the role to perfection. But he was not a member of the community, not drawn backwards and forwards by the tides of human emotion that flow in rural communities and lead to friendships, marriages, blood feuds and well attended wakes and funerals. He was an outsider, and always intended to remain one. As a recorder and observer, that is a strength.

The second area of genius was a film maker: a minor genius certainly – not a Flaherty or Riefensthal, not least because he only tried once. But a genius none the less in a small, domestic sense.

It is Kissling who perfectly captures actual life: puts nothing in front of it, does not make it perform or parade and refuses to order and confine it. The shepherds untangling the rams, the boy on his way to the peat bank, the man mending fishing line – certainly they know that they are on camera, but they would be doing what they are doing anyway and doing it in the same way, with the same swagger, or the same determination. Kissling is just there, recording and observing and then (with his editor) tying together the images to present a slice of life.

And being a coherent observer, able to create images of meaning, is no small skill. It defies some of the best professionals, and nearly all amateurs. That is why we so often have to sit through tedious home videos, or equally tedious television programmes.

In any pile of film stock, waiting to be edited or in any stack of videotapes waiting to be digitally off-lined, there are a thousand films. It is the choice of one item over another, the sequencing of one item before another, and the motion of one item to another that makes each film a set of unique choices from the material to hand. Of course the material is planned, and parts are already edited in the head: but again and again it is the choice of the moment that makes sense and takes precedence over the intentions of the past – even the recent past on a shoot.

Kissling's choice in his film (a choice in tandem with his editor, as it is today) may have, in some senses, pandered to his age and his audience but there is still within them the integrity of the observer, the desire to say 'This is how it is' and to leave the judgements to the audience. To say it, perhaps, with affection or with commitment – in the abstract – but to say it nonetheless.

Kissling's third genius applies in the narrow and very specialist field he chose for his academic study. Looking at the beautiful drawings of Alasdair and Neil Steafan, and at the modern black houses that are beginning to be built, it is a tribute to Kissling that he took the idea of the traditional Gaelic dwelling and underpinned it with enough scholarship and research that its strength and its adaptability should be attracting the enthusiasm and energy of two such talented young architects. Maybe they would have come to it anyway, but Alasdair Steafan admits that it was Kissling's work that inspired him and informed his passion.

Each of these aspects of his genius is profound, influential and significant. But each still needs to be understood in the context of his life. It is certainly apposite that Kissling finished his life in Scotland – a country he grew to love. For the Scots are fond of the flawed genius: the feet of clay which need to be attached to their heroes.

The man who made the first ever film in Gaelic; the man who recorded better than anyone else the life of the Gael before that life became integrated with the life of the Gall; the man who preserved the idea of the perfectly adapted dwelling house for a rural island population, and allowed it to be handed on – he was of the Scottish heroic mould, with his faults as visible as his virtues, yet none the waur for that!

He was self-centred, selfish, perhaps a little unfeeling and certainly able to skim over life while most plod through the mire. Yet he was also inspirational, visionary and passionately committed to the best of the past – and to preserving and injecting those good things not just into the present, but into our collective future.

In a sense he was that 'will o' the wisp' which he describes in one sequence of *A Poem of Remote Lives*. But because he needed the freedom for 'spontaneous self-expression', he wanted it to be a part of all of our lives, dancing in front of us across the moors and bogs of our daily drudgery. In some of his last written words he asked, as we have seen, 'Can we do without it?'

He knew we cannot. And whilst time and circumstances mean that few of us could live as he did, he continues to underline the need for such self-expression – and to celebrate its results – whenever we look at one of his photographs, or settle down to watch his single film.

It may be that one can only achieve the right to spontaneous self-expression by being able to be free of the commitments and entanglements of ordinary life. For many, that would be a heavy price to pay. But somehow the mixture of genes and history and serendipity allowed Werner Kissling for most of his long life to exercise his spontaneity and his self-expression, and we are the richer for it.

For all his faults, that is what made him such an attractive and engaging companion and which, I think, also made him so keen that no one should delve too deeply into his life. For beyond the dancing light and the desire to avoid being trapped, there is a hunger for the certainties of the past which he knew were slipping away for ever. He would not have wished such frailty, and such doubt, to be seen as part of his make up, although for me they make him more, rather than less attractive.

Inevitably Werner Kissling hid the deepest part of himself away from the world. That was the part that realised the show he put on, and saw that the wellspring for continual spontaneity and self-expression was a fear of something lacking in himself.

Freud would have hypothesised the kernel of that fear as being within his sexuality. In a post-Freudian age we can be more wide-ranging, and see his fear as being a product of a rigid upbringing, German pre-First World War society and the lack of purpose that inherited wealth can bring.

In a part of himself, I believe, he wished to remain at Heizendorf forever, folded in his mother's arms and distant from the troubled century he was forced to live through. But, as I said at the start of this story – I never met him, and though I have grown to know him well, I cannot say with any certainty precisely what he was like. His friends defend and protect his memory: those who have only seen his work admire him and sometimes even attempt to emulate him. And there are millions upon millions who will never even hear of him and for them his whole life and work are as alien as our time is to that of his birth.

It is time for others to come to some judgements about him, and especially about his work. I hope he would not mind his photographs being seen by a wider audience after all these years. I hope that he would appreciate his film being analysed and shown to many more people than saw it when he lived. And I hope he would – with the twinkle in his eye that David Lockwood describes – forgive me for dragging into the light not just the contents of that precious suitcase, but also his past and something of his personality. It was a necessary part of the process.

I would have liked to discuss all that with him over a dram in the comfortable bar of the Kings Arms in Melrose. And since I cannot, I apologise here and now if – in the shades – he is offended. I only did it because what he did deserves not to be forgotten, and might enthuse others as I have been enthused.

For I know that his images – rolling through my mind like the film unravelling on the plates of that Steenbeck on which I first examined it frame by frame – will always be with me and that Kissling's legacy will outlive that of many more transparent visitors to the Western Isles who have been, and seen, and then attempted to tell the story.

PART II

THE LEICA III, INTRODUCED IN 1933, WHICH KISSLING TOOK WITH HIM TO ERISKAY IN 1934

APPENDICES

The Origins of Leica and the Leica III

The actual name Leica is a combination of two names: LEI/tz CA/mera. The origins of the Leica camera stemmed from The Carl Kellner Optische Institut founded in Wetzlar, Germany in 1849. A few years later Mr Kellner engaged the services of Dr Ernst Leitz I who had come to Wetlzar from Sulzburg-Baden. The Institute was renowned for manufacturing the most precise and accurate microscopes, as Wetzlar was, and still is, a place where precision engineering flourishes.

In 1869 Carl Kellner died and Ernst Leitz purchased the Institute from his widow. By that time it had established agencies in China, Japan, Berlin, New York and St Petersburg. In 1907, Leitz delivered microscope No. 100,000 inscribed with the motto 'DO YOUR UTMOST TO DESERVE YOUR INHERITANCE'.

It was during 1911 that Mr Oskar Barnack was invited to head the Research and Development Department at E. Leitz Wetzlar and in 1914 Mr Barnack 'invented' the Leica camera. This was first exhibited at the Leipzig Spring fair in 1925 to almost universal acclaim.

In 1932, Oskar Barnack produced the Leica model II with built-in coupled rangefinder (a revolution in 35mm photography). This camera had interchangeable lenses and speeds from 1/20 sec to 1/500 sec. It took standard 35mm cine film and was built with the utmost precision to the limits of technical feasibility.

The camera was so successful that in 1933 Leitz introduced the more advanced Leica III. This had a small dial in front of the camera for shutter speeds of 1 sec to 1/20 sec, while the faster speeds from 1/20 sec to 1/500 sec were set from the shutter speed dial on the top of the camera.

It also had lateral eyelets for attaching a carrying strap and an improved rangefinder with higher magnification with dioptre correction.

The Leica III started at serial no. 107601 and production terminated in 1939 at serial no. 343100. The black models had nickel-plated controls but the chrome models had chrome controls.

The total production in black was 27,366 and in chrome was 49,091.

Captions to Part II

The identity of many of those in the portraits has been confirmed by individuals who lived on Eriskay during Kissling's visits. They have also assisted in the identification of some of those who feature in the film (for example in the portrait on page 21, which is now known to be Angus Cumming – An Cumeanach Rhuadh). Some of those photographed, however, remain unknown.

Page 71 The *Elspeth* with Eriskay in the background. A staged shot, as Kissling was the photographer.

Page 72 The approach to Eriskay as seen from the *Elspeth*.

Page 73 Acairseid Mor – the main Eriskay harbour.

Page 74 Tigh Anaoghais 'ic Eagain – beside the harbour at Acairseid Mor.

Page 75 *Rathad Kissling* (Kissling's Road) – the track which was upgraded with proceeds from the première of the film.

Page 76 The black house, a subject on which Kissling became an acknowledged expert.

Page 77 Another view of the same subject.

Page 78 Two Annas – identified as Anna Dhughaill and Anne Iagain.

Page 79 Thatching was a regular chore and required much skill and experience.

Page 80 Kissling's fascination for traditional implements emerges strongly in the film and in many of his photographs. Here hay is being gathered.

Page 81 Bean Sheonnaidh 'ic Dhonnaicheadh – Mary MacInnes along with Bean Iagain Mhoir.

Page 82 Mary MacInnes is again featured, this time at the *luadh*. Others present include Bean Iagain Mhoir (at back), Peigi Anaoghais Iain Mhic, several MacInnes sisters and Iain Alasdair.

Page 83 Women played, and play, a strong role in crofting life. Kissling would have observed this scene many times in an island summer.

Page 84 Bean Iagain Mhoir, who was the only person weaving on the island at the time of Kissling's visit. She appears in many of Kissling's photographs (including pages 94, 82 and 81, and in a still from the film on page 22) particularly as she was an expert on traditional wool crafts.

Page 85 Bean Ghilleasbaig Steaphain (Mary MacIsaac).

Page 86 The gathering of sheep for shearing and dipping involved, and still involves, neighbours, friends and the community.

Page 87 The Eriskay pony was a vital adjunct to moving peats.

Page 89 A fine study taken after the shearing.

Page 90 Donald and Peigi MacIntyre. The baskets are for carrying peat.

Page 91 Work on lobster creels was a constant task during the season.

Page 92 A picture which has strong resonances of similar rural communities in Ireland and elsewhere on the Western seaboard of Europe.

Page 93 Peigi Mhoir 'ic Mhicheal Eachainn: women constantly knitted at rest or work, and even when carrying heavy creels of peat on their backs.

Page 95 A *pladh* on the loom.

Page 96 Annag Eachainn 'ic Dhomnall.

Page 97 Seamus Gilleasbuig Steaphain, who is also in the still from the film on page 20, working with the others at the sheep fank.

Page 98 Iain MacDonald.

Page 99 Clann Anaoghais 'ic Eaghainn.

Page 100 Donnachaidh Mac Dhomnail Chailean.

Page 103 Either Iain or Dugald MacDonald.

Page 104 Seonaid Currie (née MacIntyre). According to Catriona MacKinnon she was always 'as happy as she looks there'.

Page 105 Bean Anaoghais 'ic Eaghainn (Mairi MacIntyre) with her daughters, Annie (in her arms) and Flora by her side. This photograph was identified by one of the daughters at the showing of the original slides in Eriskay in October 1995, even though it was projected the wrong way round! The children are probably first cousins of those in the photo on page 99.

Image Catalogue